START NOW!

A BOOK OF SOUL AND SPIRITUAL EXERCISES

Meditation Instructions, Meditations, Exercises,

Verses for Living a Spiritual Year, Prayers for the Dead

& Other Practices for Beginning and

Experienced Practitioners

START NOW!

A BOOK OF SOUL AND SPIRITUAL EXERCISES

*Meditation Instructions, Meditations, Exercises,
Verses for Living a Spiritual Year, Prayers for the Dead
& Other Practices for Beginning and
Experienced Practitioners*

RUDOLF STEINER

EDITED AND INTRODUCED BY
CHRISTOPHER BAMFORD

STEINERBOOKS

Published by SteinerBooks
610 Main Street
Great Barrington, MA 01230
www.steinerbooks.org

This book contains selections translated from the following volumes of the complete works (*Gesamtausgabe* [GA]) of Rudolf Steiner published by the Rudolf Steiner Nachlassverwaltung, Dornach, Switzerland: *Einleitungen zu Goethe's Naturwissenschaftlichen Schriften* (GA 1); *Die Philosophie der Freiheit* (GA 4); *Wie erlangt man Erkenntnisse der höheren Welten* (GA 10); *Die Geheimwissenschaft im Umriss* (GA 13); *Die Schwelle der geistigen Welt* (GA 17); *Wahrspruchworte* (GA 40); *Sprüche, Dichtungen, Mantren* (GA 40a); *Ursprung und Ziel des Menschen* (GA 53); *Die Welträtsel und die Anthroposophie* (GA 54); *Vor der Tore der Theosophie* (GA 95); *Anweisungen für eine esoterische Schulung* (GA 245); *Unsere Toten* (GA 261); *Zur Geschichte und aus den Inhalten der ersten Abteilung der Esoterische Schule (1904-1914)* (GA 264); *Zur Geschichte und aus den Inhalten der erkenntniskultischen Abteilung der Esoterische Schule (1904-1914)* (GA 265); *Aus den Inhalten der Esoterischen Stunden I, II, III* (GA 266/1/2/3); *Seelenübungen mit Wort- und Sinnbild-Meditationen* (GA 267); and *Mantrische Sprüche: Seelenübungen II* (GA 268). Translated with permission from the Rudolf Steiner Nachlassverwaltung, Dornach, Switzerland.

Library of Congress Cataloging-in-Publication Data

Steiner, Rudolf, 1861-1925.
  [Selections. English. 2004]
  Start now! meditation instructions, meditations, exercises, verses for living a spiritual year, prayers for the dead & other practices for beginning and experienced practitioners /Rudolf Steiner; edited and introduced by Christopher Bamford.
    p. cm.
  Includes bibliographical references.
· ISBN 0-88010-526-7 (pbk.)
  I. Anthroposophy. 2. Meditations. I. Bamford, Christopher, 1943- II. Title.
BP595.S894S6913 2004
299'.935--dc22

                                          2004001281

Printed in the United States of America

Contents

Introduction

I am not one of those who dive into the day like an animal in human form.
I pursue a quite specific goal, an idealistic aim—knowledge of the truth!
This cannot be done offhandedly. It requires the greatest striving in the world,
free of all egotism, and equally of all resignation.
— Rudolf Steiner, in a letter, July 27, 1888

1.

Rudolf Steiner (1861–1925), some of whose meditations and meditation instructions are collected here, was a truth-seeker, visionary, and seer. He was an exceptional spiritual teacher, whose unique genius was to translate into modern consciousness humanity's most ancient striving to know itself and, in knowing itself, know nature, the cosmos, and the divine. A philosopher, scientist, and esotericist, Steiner was a dedicated, servant of humanity, who gave unstintingly to the world of the wisdom he gained through the radical method of meditative, spiritual research that he inaugurated and practiced. The range of this research, far-reaching in its practical implications, included every aspect of human striving, from cosmology, evolution, and history to physics, mathematics, biology, psychology, and astronomy. On its basis, Steiner was able to make significant practical contributions to fields as diverse as education (Waldorf schools), agriculture (biodynamics), medicine (anthroposophical medicine), and social theory (the threefold social order). He was also an artist, a playwright, and an architect. As a spiritual teacher, the side of him represented here, we may say that he was the foremost exponent of the inner path of Western spirituality in the twentieth century. The movement he started, Anthroposophy, represents the growing tip of the Western spiritual traditions. Above all, he was a thinker, a world-transforming, paradigm-creating figure, often likened in his far-reaching significance to other great thinkers and world-creators like Aristotle and Thomas Aquinas. Because he was a thinker, his anthroposophical path of meditation, whatever form it took (Theosophical, philosophical, Rosicrucian, or Christian-Gnostic) was always (whether it involved thinking, feeling, or willing) *a path of knowing*. His was a cognitive path.

2

Steiner's passion to know for himself is evident in the earliest document we have from his hand, a letter written when he was nineteen (January 13, 1881):

It was the night from January 10th to the 11th. I didn't sleep a wink. I was busy with philosophical problems until about 12:30 a.m. Then, finally, I threw myself down on my couch. All my striving during the previous year had been to research whether the following statement by Schelling was true or not: "Within everyone dwells a secret, marvelous capacity to draw back from the stream of time—out of the self clothed in all that comes to us from outside—into our innermost being and there, in the immutable form of the Eternal, to look into ourselves." I believe, and I am still quite certain of it, that I discovered this capacity in myself. I had long had an inkling of it. Now the whole of idealist philosophy stands before me transformed in its essence. What's a sleepless night compared to that!

3

Any introduction to Rudolf Steiner's instructions for spiritual practice must begin with the idea of research: the experimental (experiential) pursuit of truth, based on the need to find out for oneself.

"Thinking," too, must be mentioned right at the beginning, for that is where Steiner himself began. A "cognitive" element underlies all his spiritual exercises, no matter how far from thinking (as we usually conceive of it) they appear to be. Although he does not denigrate ordinary thinking, thinking in the higher sense that Steiner uses it does not involve any kind of ratiocination, cerebration, calculation, or logical deduction. The kind of thinking Steiner aims at does not demand that the "brain" produce thoughts, but rather that it become so still that, instead of thinking in the ordinary sense, we begin to experience—to think, feel, and will—what it is "to be thought, felt, and willed." Thinking is a suprasensory, "brain-free" activity. It engages the whole person: not "I think, therefore I am," but "It thinks me."

We may call this kind of thinking *"thinking of the heart."* Steiner believed heart thinking was the next stage in humanity's ever-evolving journey of consciousness and dedicated his life and work to developing it.

4

In this sense, then, Steiner is a thinker who seeks knowledge of the truth. He seeks to be formed by the truth, to be led by it. He understands that pursuit of the truth frees us from selfishness and egoism, and that "love of truth is the only love that sets the 'I' free." Truth, for Steiner, is synonymous with reality. It is the great teacher of selflessness. Experiences of states, no matter how elevated or profound, intense or transforming, are insufficient. We must pass beyond mysticism of that kind. Experience is only the beginning of the path, which is a path of consciousness, of conscious research.

"Consciousness" by its nature witnesses and bears witness. It is "knowing with," cognizing, and witnessing. To be a good witness, one must bear witness to, and be *transformed by what one has witnessed.* Furthermore, what one has witnessed must be *communicable.* One must be able to *communicate* what one has witnessed, otherwise one's witnessing is vain and unfruitful. If consciousness does not communicate, that is, witness or testify, it betrays and forfeits the primal capacity to witness that defines human nature. For Steiner, consciousness is primary and communicates. Like any good witness, it is free, independent, and transparent, uncontaminated by preconceptions of any kind.

Unlike the legal witness who is passive, the spiritual witness is *active,* engaged. Rather than just happening to be there, the spiritual seeker as witness seeks to find out. Indeed, perhaps the basic meaning of a spiritual (or esoteric) path is to find out for oneself. The exoteric, or outer, vehicle provides the basic teachings. It contains information about the visible and invisible worlds — that the human being is made up of body, soul, and spirit; that Christ was God and that he incarnated in a human body to redeem humanity from sin; that all beings have Buddha nature; that the Earth passed through three previous evolutionary stages called Saturn, Sun, and Moon and will pass through three more; and so on. One can certainly understand these with ordinary consciousness. Ordinary thinking can determine—"by their fruits ye shall know them"—whether they make sense, and whether they seem healthy and life-enhancing. But unless one finds out for oneself, they remain mere theories to be taken on faith. There is nothing wrong with doing so. If one has determined that the teachings are "good" and, accordingly, leads one's as if they were true, one will lead a better life. Some people, however, need to find out for themselves. They begin a meditative path.

5

There is no mystery about meditation.

Before you begin, you must select a meditation theme or practice—something that interests you, the layers of whose meaning you wish to explore. This may be a verse or line of Rudolf Steiner or of any spiritual or mystical literature from the Upanishads to an alchemical text (for example, a Gospel text or a line from Meister Eckhart). Or, it may be an image or symbol like the Rose Cross, the Caduceus, or Ouroboros—or a cosmological diagram from some old alchemical book. Or, again, it may be some natural or fabricated object (a pebble or a pin), or even a symbolic gesture like the sign of the Cross, holding the palms together, or outstretching the arms. It may even be a question that has come to you, or that you have formulated. Once you have decided—let us say that you have chosen the theme "Wisdom lives in the Light"— you are ready to begin.

It is best to choose a peaceful time of the day. Find a quiet place where you will not be disturbed. Pick a comfortable chair, one that feels good to you, that you feel at home in, and where your back can be reasonably straight and your feet rest easily on the floor. Place a pen and notebook beside you. If you wish, and are used to it, you may sit on a cushion on the floor. There are no rules. The attitude is experimental. See what works. Find out what happens. Once you are seated, take a few deep breaths to relax. Relax your face, your neck and shoulders, your chest area, your stomach, your legs and feet. Let your hands rest lightly on your thighs or in your lap. Again, whatever feels comfortable. Settle in. Feel at home, at peace with yourself and the world. Think to yourself: "Now I am going to begin my meditation." Relax your mouth into a half-smile, breathe lightly and easily, and allow the thoughts and memories of the day to dissipate slowly. Fill yourself with a mood of reverence or devotion by orienting yourself momentarily to the higher worlds—to God, or the angels, or whatever is highest for you. Now, carefully place the chosen phrase in the center of your consciousness. Think around it, taking each word in turn, as well as the sentence as a whole, pondering, associating, and amplifying until you feel you have, for the moment, exhausted the possibilities. Now, collapse the sentence into one of its words. For instance, collapse "Wisdom lives in the Light" into the word "Light." Then concentrate all that you have associated, pondered, and amplified into a single beam of attention and focus it on the whole sentence condensed into the word "Light." Keep your attention as focused as possible. If you are distracted or wander off, simply return to the theme and refocus. Do this for as long as feels comfortable (or you sense your attention tiring). Then, when it feels right, release the sentence so that your mind is empty. Try to keep it empty as long as possible. See what happens, what comes down. If images occur, follow them and let them unfold. After a short period, at a certain moment in this process, you will feel a natural closure occurring. You will feel that the meditation is ending. Let it end. Sit quietly. At an appropriate moment, say to yourself, "Now the meditation is over." Reach for your notebook, and write down whatever seemed noteworthy to you about what just happened. As for distractions, they are to be expected. If your mind wanders off, as it will, do not be discouraged (even if this happens repeatedly and continuously), simply return to the theme of your meditation.

6

Such meditation has a long history in the West. Though Rudolf Steiner never referred to any sources, and though he also (as part of his Theosophical heritage) drew on and practiced various Eastern, particularly Yogic, disciplines, the method he taught clearly belongs to the Abrahamic traditions of the Book. Two examples come to mind.

First, there is the monastic practice of *lectio divina*, or sacred, slow, contemplative reading. The reading and learning by heart of sacred texts lay at the heart of Christian spiritual practice from earliest times, but it was not "formalized" until the twelfth century, when Guigo, a Carthusian, described reading as a four-step ladder connecting Earth to heaven. He called these steps or stages: *lectio* (or reading), *meditatio* (or meditation), *oratio* (or prayer), and *contemplatio* (or contemplation).

Lectio is slow, reflective, thorough reading and re-reading, word by word, sentence by sentence, sometimes only completing one or two in the allotted time. You read as if God were speaking to you. You read with your heart. You listen over and over again to the words, straining to hear what is being said, what God means and wants from you.

Entering the stage of *meditatio* or meditation, you begin to ruminate, ponder, associate, and think around God's word, as if it were addressed directly and only to you, questioning your own life. One thinks here of Rilke's famous poem on the Archaic Torso of Apollo: *you must change your life.*

With *oratio* or prayer, you stop thinking, and simply remain with your heart open. This is the moment of the heart's response to what you have experienced up to now. Finally, in *contemplatio* (contemplation), you let go of everything. You empty yourself completely and simply rest in pure, empty, *listening.*

The second example comes from the Hermetic, alchemical lineage of those whom Steiner calls "the old philosophers." This "Rosicrucian" tradition was also text-based, similar in many ways to *lectio divina.* In this case, the texts are esoteric, dense, symbolic, occult, paradoxical allegories, containing the most profound understanding of creation and nature expressed in radically nondual language. Anyone who has ever tried to read an alchemical text knows how difficult it is to penetrate and understand even the first glimmers of the wisdom it contains. There is only one way. *Lege, lege, ora, et lege:* Read, read, pray, and read again. By "reading"— what Steiner in his description of the Rosicrucian path calls "study"—is meant something very close to the kind of meditation underlying Steiner's teaching.

Here we should not forget that, for Steiner, as for the monks and the old alchemical philosophers of nature, *everything is text.* The cosmos is a vast, polysemous, multileveled "book." It is to be read, as everything else is to be read: stars, faces, hands, flowers, rocks. St. Anthony, when asked by some visitors, "Sir philosopher, what do you do, deprived as you are of books to be read in your desert retreat?" answered: "I read the Book of Nature." Reading in the book of nature, which is not an activity different in kind from the reading of a sacred text, lies at the center of Steiner's vision of a renewal of cosmic intelligence in our time. Reading, when Steiner speaks of it, should never be taken in the narrow sense of referring to books alone, but as human cognitive activity engaged in active, redeeming perception of the world.

7

Such meditation should be done regularly and persistently. Working with the same meditation repeatedly deepens the experience, which is always new (never the same). One never exhausts a meditation; and there is no telling how long one must persevere before a satisfactory, though always provisional, result is reached. It is important to realize, too, that, although a meditation is formally restricted to its fifteen minutes, after which we return to our unimpeded daily tasks, informally, once a meditation is begun, its questioning continues to live spiritually through the days and months, and we never know when an insight will come. As Steiner says (in *Christ and the Spiritual World*), "If research is to reveal a truth that by its nature imparts the conviction of its rightness, *we must be guided slowly and by stages.* This ensures that we are not enticed into speculation or fantasy realms that lead us away from the truth we are seeking." Thus it often seems that one is held back or delayed. There can be dry periods. But every now and then, like showers in a time of drought, landmarks appear to let us know that our task has not been forgotten. Insights may and do come, but, if we are honest, we must recognize that for the most part they are only way stations and not yet (very rarely) the goal. The clues we receive from our meditation are like parables: They reveal their true significance only gradually. When something more conclusive does finally come, Steiner points out, it is often in connection both with our karma and with something apparently unrelated to our chief concern.

Meditation or spiritual research of this kind does not take place in a vacuum. It requires a medium in which to exist and a place and an environment to support it. Its site is our very own human life, which engages us as whole persons of body, soul, and spirit. We live this Earthly life as human beings in interdependence with other human beings, with whom we constitute humanity, as well as with the numberless other beings (mineral, plant, animal, and spiritual) who make up our planet. Our task, which is the Earth's too, for we are one with her, is *love*—to transform the Earth into love. The medium of our meditation is thus the life of the heart; it is our moral life. Rudolf Steiner never tires of repeating the Golden Rule that one must take many moral steps forward to advance one step in knowledge. By this, he does not mean following any abstract code of behavior, but rather bringing loving consciousness and attention to our everyday lives and relationships. To do so is to begin to awaken to the soul's own true nature—which is moral through and through. It is to begin to awaken the soul faculties that we call virtues. A virtue is not something we do but is a power of the soul. To practice a virtue is to empower the soul. Steiner refers to many virtues, well-known to all, but ignored or excluded by our egotism. Underlying all is the ancient, primordial sense of reverence for, and devotion to, the divine. The sense of awe and wonder is fundamental, for it teaches us reverence as such. For the modern age, St. Francis (as Steiner shows in his little book *The Spiritual Foundations of Morality*) engendered a threefold translation of reverence into the interpersonal realm, making it ethical in a groundbreaking sense. His first insight was to extrapolate faith in the divine into faith in the divine ground of each soul, with the result that everyone he met was, in essence, divine. On this basis, he then experienced and taught a new, boundless love for humanity as a whole, its being, in which each of us participates in unique and irreplaceable ways. This led him to the unshakable conviction that (as Steiner puts it) every soul may be guided back to the divine-spiritual worlds that are its and our true home. From these derive the basic practices of gratitude (the other face of reverence), forgiveness, openness, and solidarity and community with all life, as well as "simpler" practices like listening (non-judgment and impartiality), equanimity, self-control, control of thought, and so on. Steiner called these "supplementary" exercises, for they should accompany or supplement all meditation.

Meditation is thus concerned with two irrevocably intertwined mysticisms: the mysticism of human encounter and the mysticism of the self. The struggle against egotism—the struggle to become selfless—lies at the heart of both.

8

But why meditate at all? The reasons are paradoxical.

As Steiner often stresses, meditation is the only completely free act we can do. When we meditate, we perform a free act. Nothing compels us to meditate. Purposive "effort" is also out of place. We should meditate as a plant flowers, naturally, spontaneously, effortlessly, without ego, not because there is a reason to do so, but because *we* choose to: just because. To meditate is a free decision, a free deed of consciousness. As a free act, meditation is ideally (this is the non-aim) not only not purposive, it is without an object. Georg Kühlewind refers to "form-free attention," by which he means "thinking without a thought" or an object of thought. At the same time, because it is free and we do it, it changes us. In other words, through meditation, we *become*. We become true subjects.

Meditation is also, and necessarily, playful.

Therefore, in the world's terms, meditation like art is superfluous, even useless. It serves no practical end. Life goes on very well without it. It will not necessarily make us either rich, healthy, or happy. Yet, it is the most important thing we can do in life. Like art, it gives life *meaning*.

This gift of meaning is a free gift of our creativity, given out of "poverty of spirit," without any expectation of reward.

It follows that meditation is an experience of grace. It allows us to experience that *everything is given*: "every good and perfect gift is from above and cometh down from the Father of lights (James 1:17)."

All this means that, when we meditate, we start from nothing. Every meditation re-enacts the opening of St. John's Gospel: *In the beginning*. We always begin anew, from nothing. Yet, like art (as a form of art), meditation is the true source of love, because it allows us to intuit what is not yet and thereby begin to give it birth. Meditation is our most creative act.

So, we could say that when we meditate, we do so not for ourselves but for the sake of the spiritual world. Meditating, we become coworkers with God and his angels who can work with us directly only through our freedom, our human-angelic nature. This freedom, as theology explains, is *the freedom to turn*. From that freedom, all other free acts flow. Because our meditation arises from our freedom, it causes great joy in the spiritual world. The angels suffer with us in our fallenness, our unfreedom; but when we act freely, they rejoice in the recovery of our angelic nature. For them, our meditation is truly a gift, in the giving of which we receive much more than we give: participation in the evolving creative goodness of the world. When we meditate, therefore, we change the world.

Therefore, when we meditate, we begin to fulfil our human vocation as the "tenth hierarchy," collaborators with the Seraphim, Cherubim, Thrones, Dominions, Virtues, Powers, Principalities, Archangels, and Angels, as well as the whole exalted company of beings in the spiritual world that includes all saints and masters, gods and goddesses.

Meditation may, of course, make us more serene and peaceful; it may make us more able to gain some measure of self-control and detachment. If we meditate, we may be better able to deal with life's inevitable ups and downs. We may even, as a result of meditating over a long period of time, gain certain soul capacities that allow us to confirm for ourselves what the great spiritual teachings affirm. But these are not, in fact, reasons for meditating. If we make them reasons, then our meditation will probably disappoint our intentions. Above all, meditation is to seek, without end—to become a question.

9

As a free deed, meditation is naturally individual, uniquely our own. It is where we most fully *become* ourselves. Its practice is also always individual. There are no rules. Just as every potter will elaborate his or her own way of making pots, so every meditant will shape his or her own meditation. No two people will do a given meditation in exactly the same way. The same meditation practiced daily will be different every time. Every meditation is experimental. One never knows what is going to happen. Part of the joy is watching, waiting, and witnessing what happens. Improvisation is essential. After all, we are not passive in this experiment. *We* are the subject, the active participant in what will happen. There is no "wrong" way of doing the meditation, except not doing it! Steiner was always leery of imposing too strict or formal an instruction. When counseling someone, often he would lay out tentatively, even hesitantly, the meditation's framework and parameters, with some indication of a theme. Then he would give advice as to how the meditation might be carried out, adding, "But suit it to yourself," or words to that effect. "Meditation advice" is thus more accurate than "meditation instruction." *Meditation is something to play with.*

While meditation is a free, individual act in which we are most ourselves, at the same time it leads us out of our ordinary everyday selves and allows us to begin to experience the least subjective, most universal aspect of who we are: our attention. All meditation is an exercise in attention, whether it is thinking attention, feeling attention, or willing attention. And attention, which in its purest form we may call "thinking (or consciousness) without an object," gives us our first taste of the true "I." In this sense, meditation is the art of self-knowledge.

10

Spiritual teachers have walked the path they teach step by step. There is nothing theoretical about their work. They know; and their knowledge is the matured fruit of lifetimes, cooked and transformed in the crucible of this present life with all its joy and suffering. They are exceptional human beings. We may call them *initiates*. R. A. Schwaller de Lubicz gives an interesting and quite useful explanation of the double working involved in the provenance of an initiate's knowledge (and, in some sense, anyone's spiritual knowledge) in the introduction to lectures he gave on his teaching (*La Doctrine*, 1926):

Above all, I inherited it as one inherits one's blood. What I established through many struggles and nights of research is, in fact, only knowledge I possessed in a past life. The effort I made was an effort to unveil, not to acquire. But there is no merit in that; for the reward far surpasses any suffering or effort. However, this is only one aspect of the question. The other is *revelation*, a word often used without knowledge of its true import. Revelation is not inspiration, a sudden bedazzlement. It is a veritable giving birth. As in the case of a mother, for whom the natural term indicates the moment when the birth should occur, which then happens with all the pains of an effort demanded by necessity but refused by the body through inertia, so the light of "revelation" enters the world.

One feels revelation coming, one knows the moment has arrived when an obscure but powerful desire will realize itself; one feels it coming despite all the incredible obstacles that life and the occult forces know to put in its way. Once one has lived through the experience, it is strange to look back over the mountains that rose up to lead one away from the event that sought to happen, that one longed for and feared at the same time. Then the sufferings come, that is, the renunciations, the shatterings of the ego, the denial of all that one wishes for, the very offering of one's life to attain this moment when the spiritual fruit will be born. And there is another thing that one can hardly realize: you are both what receives the revelation and, like the mother, you are the one who knows least about the nature of what is revealed. Revelation occurs in a longer or shorter time, with more or less suffering, and one remains before it, astonished that it is there, and not yet understanding its meaning. Is that revelation? Not yet. You must nourish the child, learn to know it, study it under all aspects, see where and how it is ill. One is so imperfect, so ill-suited, to bring spirit into the world that the revelation runs the risk of being sickly. You want something so much, you are in such revolt against the spiritual world, you so much want to be yourself, that the process of revelation can well bring organic weaknesses into your constitution. Therefore you must now begin the real work, which is like a true maternity.

There is nothing quite comparable in Rudolf Steiner, who rarely spoke of himself in such terms. However, in a lecture on Goethe's Rosicrucian poem "The Mysteries," speaking of Brother Mark, the initiate hero of the poem, he describes what he calls "a process occurring in human life in which the highest ideas, thoughts and conceptions are transformed into feelings and perceptions." Explaining how this transformation occurs, Steiner says:

> We live through many embodiments, from incarnation to incarnation. In each, we learn many things, each full of opportunities for gathering new experiences. We cannot carry everything over in every detail from incarnation to incarnation. When we are born again, it is not necessary for everything we have learned to come to life in every detail. But if we have learned a great deal in one incarnation, and then die and are born again, although there is no need for all our ideas to live again, we come to life with the fruits of our former life, the fruits of what we have learned. Our powers of perception and feeling are in accord with our earlier incarnations.

Steiner goes on to describe how Goethe in his poem shows us "the highest wisdom, which is a fruit of former knowledge." He says that Brother Mark, the new leader of the twelve, "has transformed this knowledge into feeling and experience and is therefore qualified to lead others who have perhaps learned more in the form of concepts." Rudolf Steiner was such a leader and initiate. We should be both awed and encouraged by this. Steiner was an extraordinary, exceptional being, one of the "hidden pillars" of humanity, yet, from the perspective of reincarnation, we are all initiates. For us, too, the fruits of our former lives are available inchoately in our feelings and perceptions, if only we awake and start now on a path of inner development.

11

What is the difference between a saint and an initiate, who works assiduously at self-development for the sake of the Earth over many lifetimes? A simple, but in many respects misleading answer, is that initiates are self-made, while saints are made by God. This is misleading because the dynamic between nature and grace, or what is known in Buddhism as "own power" and "other power," is complex and ambiguous. Nature from one perspective is grace from another. Put another way: One never ascends higher by nature than grace descends. They are two sides of a single coin: God's two hands. Nevertheless, there is always a difference of emphasis. Citing a Rosicrucian legend, Rudolf Steiner frequently differentiates between what he calls, following the Biblical story of Adam's two children, the "Abel" stream and the "Cain" stream. According to Steiner, the original Adam, who was male-female, "divided into two types in his offspring, one more masculine, the other more feminine." For Steiner they represent two types of humanity or orders of service. "Abel was a keeper of sheep, but Cain was a tiller of the ground." Cain worked the Earth. He represents a bottom-up approach. He works out of himself, transforming the Earth toward heaven, offering up what he has achieved out of his own freedom by his own effort and intelligence. He creates arts and sciences, which have their roots in the Earth. As Steiner says, "The physical is the mark of Cain." Abel, on the other hand, tends what he has *received*: He is the receptive and devoted nurturer of the spirit bestowed on him by the spiritual world. Abel is the child of God, but Cain is the child of the Earth. From these, two approaches to the spirit arise. Abel's approach descends from God; Cain's rises from the human Earth. Through the sequence of Earth lives, human beings work to transform the Earth into a living divine-human-Earthly Sun for the glory of God. One is the path of the warrior or king (the Royal Art), the other the sacerdotal, or priestly path. As initiations, the one unfolds the so-called Lesser Mysteries (of the human being and the cosmos), the other the so-called Greater Mysteries (of God). One is the lineage of Cain, Tubal Cain (the primal smith who taught the use and working of metal ores and iron), Methuselah (who invented the primal Tau script), and Hiram, the architect of Solomon's temple. This line continues through the alchemists, mystical philosopher, and realized occultists, or initiates, of all ages. The other is the divine priestly lineage of Seth and Solomon, and the great company of saints formed by God. Ultimately, of course, such distinctions are untenable. We must unite both sorts of striving in ourselves. We are all called both to be saints—indeed we are already saints *potentially*—and to work the Earth and create ourselves by our own efforts. But there is always a question of emphasis. And for Steiner his path was clear: It was the Cain path, to be walked by and out of himself. His life is exemplary of his approach. Yet he sought also to reconcile the two paths and foresaw their future union.

In fact, there is no better introduction to the spiritual method Steiner taught than to meditate the life he lived. Whatever he encountered, from his earliest years to his death, was for him a spiritual exercise through which he could grow in consciousness, in knowledge of the truth, and in the practice of goodness. One thing, however, must be understood. What is most important is often unstated. Reading the story of Steiner's biography, even in his own words, could well leave the impression that knowledge of the spirit came easily to him. But this would be a misapprehension. Though by temperament typically Viennese in his sociability, congeniality, and sense of humor (and never losing the deep pleasure good company and companionship gave him), Steiner was an ascetic in (and for the sake of) his spiritual life. He dedicated himself body and soul to the mission he was given, and renounced the ordinary creature comforts of family and intimacy. In a word: He worked extremely hard (and suffered greatly) to merit the spiritual treasures he received. He does not speak of any of this, but one need only read between the lines of his texts and of his face to see that this is so.

12

Rudolf Steiner was born in obscurity in 1861 in the tiny railway town of Kraljevec, in present day Croatia, on the western edge of the vast Hungarian plain. His father was a minor railroad official, subject to the whims of bureaucracy. Thus, when Steiner was six months old, the family was sent to a town near Vienna. After six months, they were moved again to the country station of Pottschach in Lower Austria, near the Styrian border. There, for the next eight years, Steiner was formed. Majestic peaks soared in the blue distance, intimate nature gently cradled the village, and through it all ran the railroad and telegraph, which served the local mills and factories. Also present was the Catholic Church, especially in the form of a friendly priest who, though Steiner's father was a freethinker, became an intimate of the family.

Given the speed at which time is now moving, Steiner's year of birth can seem very distant indeed. Yet, appearances notwithstanding, despite the nineteenth century trappings of his life, particularly evident in some of his language and the contemporary movements (occult, Theosophical, and political) within which he moved, Rudolf Steiner is nevertheless surprisingly modern, even postmodern. Growing up between nature and technology, with a deep feeling for both, as well as for the spiritual world, he was attuned to the evolutionary possibilities each contained. He saw clearly what was lacking for creative participation in a truly human future. In other words, he saw, and oriented himself toward, where we are now.

Initially, thinking and the inner world that opened into the spiritual worlds came almost more naturally to Steiner than the physical world. By the time he was eight, when the family moved to Neudorfl on the Lower Austrian border, he already knew the difference between, as he puts it in his *Autobiography*, "things and beings that are visible and those that are invisible." He already understood thoughts not as representations of outer reality, but as "revelations of a spiritual world on the stage of the soul." Geometry, which he loved, he felt was the proof of this. We produce it inwardly, but its significance is independent of us. It seemed to him to confirm the truth of other inward perceptions.

It also fascinated him by its connections to higher mathematics and natural science, which seemed to him to pose questions and propose answers, in which he sensed some fundamental lack. Not knowing whether this lack lay in him or the subject, he elected science as his major course of study.

There were other "perceptions," or, more accurately, feelings, that were not of the visible world. We could call them clairvoyant or "psychic." For instance, one day he was sitting in one of his favorite hiding places, the railway waiting room. He saw the door open and a woman enter who was unknown to him but nonetheless resembled a member of his family. She walked to the middle of the room and, gesturing, said in effect, "Help me as much as you can." For a while, she continued to gesture. Then she went over to the stove and disappeared into it. Later, he heard that a distant relative had committed suicide and he understood that it was her soul that had visited him in search of succor. The ramifications of such an event, when experienced consciously, are profound: one knows one lives in the spiritual world. As Steiner says, speaking of himself in the third person, in a lecture entitled "Self-Education" (February 4, 1913):

> Beginning with that event, a life began to develop in the boy's soul that thoroughly revealed to him not only the worlds from which outer trees and mountains speak to the human soul, but also the worlds behind them. From that moment, the boy lived with the spirits of nature.... He lived with the creative beings behind things, and he allowed them to work upon him in the same way as he allowed the outer world to work upon him.

The young Steiner thus lived on two levels. On the one hand, the spiritual world was a reality to him; on the other, with a free and independent spirit, he threw himself into his school studies. In *how* he brought these together, we see the life of spiritual exercises to which he would dedicate himself in the process of being born. We witness, that is, the birth of an experimental consciousness, determined to uncover provisional truths, through prolonged thought or meditation either on the truths presented by any given subject or on the fundamental questions or riddles that it posed. We see him, inspired by a favorite geometry teacher, spending hours drawing with compass, ruler, and triangle, using the opportunity "to grapple with the phenomena of the sensory world to gain a perspective of the spiritual world that was naturally visible before me." Doing so, he strove for a new kind of thinking: "one capable of grasping the true nature of physical phenomena." Studying Immanuel Kant, he sought not only to understand the philosopher, but also to maintain harmony in himself between such thinking and religious teaching. For this, thinking had to become "a power that truly includes the things and processes of the world." In the same vein, he became interested in a series of books on learning mathematics independently. Thus, he taught himself analytical geometry and trigonometry, as well as differential and integral calculus. All these, we might say, were preliminary exercises, aimed at proving for himself that "the activity in human thinking is in fact spirit."

By this time, he was ready to enter the Institute of Technology in Vienna. His master was now Fichte, Kant's successor in the lineage of German idealism. Fichte led him to understand that the human "I" is the only possible starting point for knowledge, deepening his meditative life by the addition of self-observation. From Fichte, he understood that something spiritual is present in consciousness when the "I" actively observes its activity. Such observation had to be precise and communicable in clear concepts. Page by page, he rewrote Fichte's *Science of Knowledge*. Previously, he had sought to find the "I" by starting from natural phenomena. Now he sought to find natural phenomena by starting from the "I." Living in the "I," which is itself spirit, a spiritual being, he now lived in the world of spiritual beings. "The spiritual world was an immediate reality." But he could not reconcile this experience with physical nature. Therefore, it became his task to do so.

To prepare him, destiny led him to Felix Kogutski, a factory worker and mystical herb gatherer. With this apparently simple "man of the people," Steiner finally found someone with whom to discuss his spiritual experiences. Kogutski, who gathered medicinal plants and sold them in the pharmacies of Vienna, became an important teacher. Steiner says that although he had read many books on mysticism, when Kogutski spoke, elemental creative wisdom flowed from his soul, not book learning. He was one who "artlessly let stream into his heart each revelation as it came." When he entered his inmost heart, observing nature around about him, knowledge lived in him that "did not seek for words," but could be communicated in other ways. Under his tutelage, Steiner learned to "look deeply into the secrets of nature." Many years later, Steiner would repay his Kogutski by depicting him in his mystery dramas in the character Felix Balde, "the man with the lamp." Asked what must be done to give the powers of Earth what they so sorely need, Balde replies:

> As long as only those
> Find hearing on Earth
> Who will not recall
> Their spiritual source,
> The lords of metal ores
> Will hunger in the Earth's depths.

> — *The Portal of Initiation*

Later, he says more optimistically:

> We stand at a turning point in time.
> Some part of spiritual knowledge
> Who wills to open mind and heart to it
> Must be unlocked for everyone.

> — *The Souls' Probation*

Kogutski was "an emissary." He led Rudolf Steiner to a mysterious figure Steiner refers to, in the so-called "Barr Document" he wrote for Edouard Schuré, only as "the M" (Master): "I did not meet the M. immediately, but first an emissary who was completely initiated into the secrets of plants and their effects, and into their connection with the cosmos and human nature. Contact with the spirits of nature was something self-evident to him, about which he talked without enthusiasm, thereby arousing enthusiasm all the more." The precise identity of the Master is unknown, for Steiner never spoke of him directly. Tradition has it, however, that he was the initiate Christian Rosenkreutz. From him, Steiner received the directive to build a bridge from modern scientific consciousness to cognition of the spiritual world.

His primary guide in this was to be Johann Wolfgang von Goethe, the great German poet, dramatist, and novelist. Goethe was to be another initiator. Steiner was led to study him seriously by Karl Julius Schröer, his professor of German language and literature. Besides Goethe, Schröer also introduced Steiner to the living elements of German and Austro-Hungarian legend and folklore, including the famous "paradise" Christmas plays, often still performed today in Waldorf schools. Schröer was an idealist. For him, the driving force in evolution was the world of ideas. For Steiner, however, the life of the spirit lay behind the ideas. Ideas were only "shadows" of the spirit. Heated arguments ensued. When they discussed "folk souls," they seemed closer together. Often, conversation on the relationship between the spiritual and the physical worlds would take them late into the night. Schröer was finishing his introduction to *Faust* for a new collected edition of Goethe's works. *Faust* was, of course, literature. Goethe's non-dual understanding of nature and spirit was more naked in his scientific works, which, as Schröer recognized, it was Steiner's destiny to edit. Therefore he arranged for Steiner to be asked to do so (1882).

Goethe had created an alternative, participatory scientific method based not on theory or mathematics, but on direct, phenomenological observation of nature. For Steiner, what Goethe had achieved in the organic realm was the equivalent of what Galileo had done for the inorganic realm. Goethe did not come to this achievement unaided, which would be important for Steiner, too. Informing Goethe's approach was a radical transformation of the science of alchemy. Steiner's first task (the complete introductions would take him more than ten years) was to work through the idea of *metamorphosis*, as is expressed, for example, in the plant's transformational genesis from seed to seed, a process that unfolds through leaf, bud, flower, pistil and stamen, and fruit. As Steiner puts it, in this alchemical process, "in the progressing, living transformation of concepts, images arise that display the being formed in nature." But how does one conceive of the guiding entity, the archetypal plant leaf, *in* the metamorphosing plant? Or the "archetypal human" in the larger evolutionary story? This demanded a different way of *cognizing*, or knowing. No such epistemology existed, so Steiner had to create it.

Encountering Goethe, therefore, engaged Steiner even more deeply in the cultivation of his philosophical and his esoteric life. Doing so aided him immensely. Meditative experience had led him to the experience of thinking as a direct experience of reality, which, because it was completely experienced, was *certain and immune to doubt* in a way that the sensory world was not. What was the relationship between thinking, with its certainty, and the sensory world with its doubt? As Steiner oscillated between the two, he came to conclude that it was through thinking that the sensory world expressed its true nature. They were not two, but one. In this, he learned much from the philosopher Hegel's writings, which he read as meditative texts. Hegel impressed him; he had certainly achieved living thinking. But Steiner was also repelled by Hegel, because he had not allowed this experience to lead him to a concrete world of spirit. Goethe went further. *He understood that what we usually divide into subjective and objective experience could be intuited as a whole by thinking purified of preconceptions.* Through such intuitions, Goethe was able to penetrate the spiritual world.

Steiner was also involved during this period with the cultural avant-garde, including Nietzscheans, feminists, and forward-thinking Catholic thinkers, as well as early Theosophists and occultists like Friedrich Eckstein. All of these helped deepen his sense of mission and his understanding of his time and place.

Eckstein, or "Eck," was a Wagnerite, a vegetarian, a philosopher of symbolism, an alchemist, and a musician. After the M, he was the next significant spiritual influence. He introduced Steiner to the Western esoteric tradition. Steiner wrote in 1890: "There are two events in my life that I count among the most important. About one I must remain silent. The second is the circumstance that I came to know [Eckstein]." For a number of years, he guided Steiner in the understanding of the symbolic language of ancient and Hermetic texts and helped him unlock much of what Goethe had likewise expressed "symbolically." They read Goethe's poems together as well as alchemical and other esoteric texts. The few letters extant between them indicate the level of work and friendship they engaged in. For instance (1888):

Dear Mr. Steiner,
Since I absolutely need the book today, for the moment I will just note down the details and bring the book to the Coffee Shop on Monday.

The title of the book in question is: *Remarks upon Alchemy and the Alchemists*. It appeared anonymously, printed in Boston by Crosby, Nichols, and Co., 1857. The author's name, as I know from a certain source, was [Ethan Allen] Hitchcock. On page 87, we find:

Nearly all of the writers quote a saying attributed to old Ostanes, that "*nature unites by nature; nature rejoices in nature; nature improves nature; nature loves nature; nature overcomes nature; nature perfects nature; nature contains and is contained by nature,*" and several of them caution their readers to keep these principles in mind.

... I will probably not be going to the café tomorrow. But I hope to see you there on Monday.

In 1890, we find Steiner writing to Eckstein, desperate for guidance in understanding two lines from Goethe's poem "The Bride of Corinth": "Salt and Water do not cool / Where youth feels."

Eckstein replies in full. He sees the symbolism in the context of the "bride," that is, the union of male and female principles (day and night, consciousness and unconsciousness, etc.). He invokes Christian ritual. *Salt* and *water* are both primary Christian symbols. A Catholic baptism is actually incomplete if those to be baptized do not have a grain of salt laid upon their tongues while the priest says the ritual words, "*Accipe salem sapientiae, ut habeas vitam aternam*" (Take the salt of wisdom in order to have eternal life). He goes on to tell Steiner to consult Ezekiel 16. All in all, he confesses:

> The esoteric meaning of salt and water is very difficult to communicate. *Water* purifies the human Augean stables. Hercules conducts Eurotas through the Augean stables. Why Hercules? Why the Augean stables. Read everything in the bible on "the water of life," Noah, etc., and on "rain," also Goethe's poem "Legends."... *Salt* is a primordial symbol for spiritual resurrection and immortality. *Salt* arises when wood is burned and the ash is leached out. Salt is matter that is clarified. It obeys only the pure mathematical law of spheres, leaving everything unclean behind in the mother liquor. Otherwise the flesh retains its rottenness. But God has sealed the elect with a *bond of salt*, as the Bible says.

Besides the traditional realms of alchemy and occultism, Eckstein, who had met Madame Blavatsky, also introduced Steiner to Theosophy and streams related to it. Steiner took note. For the moment, apparently, he felt no affinity. Certainly, A. P. Sinnett's *Esoteric Buddhism* struck him as displaying many errors and no great depth of thought. Besides, he had philosophical and preparatory work to do.

To this, he dedicated the immediate future. None of it was theoretical. Whatever he undertook was practical, existential, and initiatory. Over the next years, Steiner by his own effort, meditation, study, and suffering would realize the full power of the true "I."

13

Central to the work of the "I" is *The Philosophy of Freedom* (translated as *Intuitive Thinking as a Spiritual Path*). It is the work which, when asked which of his books he would most want rescued if some catastrophe should strike, Steiner always unhesitatingly named. Upon its basis all the rest, the whole vast edifice of Anthroposophy, could be recreated. It is no ordinary book. Each line arises from Steiner's own personal experience. It is a record of his spiritual journey and, in that sense, also a manual (for those able to follow it inwardly) of spiritual practice for us.

Following its publication, he wrote to his friend Rosa Mayreder (November 1894):

I do not *teach*. I recount what I experienced inwardly. Everything in my book is personal, even the shape of the thoughts. Someone fond of teaching might expand on the theme. I myself may do so one day. But my first wish was to show *the biography of a soul struggling to freedom*. There is nothing you can do in such circumstances to help those who insist on joining you in scaling cliff faces and crossing abysses. It's all you can do to get across yourself. The inner urge to cross burns too strongly to allow for stopping and explaining to others how they might find the easiest way there. I took my own path and followed it as well as I was able. This was the path I described.... My interest in philosophy is restricted almost entirely to the experience of the individual.

But not just any individual. Steiner is the individual who discovers what it means to *think* and *to think independently*, outside the box. Discovering in the experience of thinking that when we think we are the universe, he discovers the true freedom of thinking. This is not thinking as "having thoughts," but actual non-dual being, beyond subject and object, inside and outside, concept and percept. It is not the conceptual husk by which we habitually know the world, but the living tip, or outer fringe, of the universal flow itself. To experience this is to experience the impossible: that we are co-creators, resurrectors, of the world. It is to think things through to the end. Ultimately, it is to commune with, and perceive, intuit, the essence of things, the universal spirit. It is to enter the spiritual world. Dead thinking crucifies the world. To the extent that we move from thoughts to the formative life of thinking and thinking becomes alive in us, we resurrect it. The world is resurrected. We can accomplish this only one by one—individually. As Steiner wrote in his introductions to Goethe's scientific writings, "Truth is always only the individual truth of significant human beings."

14

The period between the ages of thirty-six and forty (1897–1901) was critical to Steiner in a different way and led to his stepping onto the world stage as a spiritual teacher. First, having always lived in the spiritual world, he now began to live in and understand the sensory, physical world. His ability to observe physical processes and beings became more accurate and penetrating. He understood that the sensory world, including the world of human beings, could reveal something that only it could reveal. He also experienced how the physical world leads directly into the spiritual. All this led in a surprising way to the realization: The world is full of mysteries that are not to be solved by thoughts. Rather, the phenomenon of a mystery reveals itself in the reality that it is. At the same time he understood that the real key to all mysteries was humanity, the human being, itself. *The world is the question; the human being is the answer.* Or rather, the stage upon which the answer appears.

Second, underlying the above, Steiner learned "through *inner experience*, the nature of meditation and its significance for understanding the spiritual realm." As he himself says, "I had led a meditative life before then.... But now something arose within me that demanded meditation as an absolute necessity for my soul life." Such meditation, he found, led to the participation and union of the whole person in and with the spiritual world. More than that, he discovered that meditation led to an awareness of an "inner human spirit" that could live within the spiritual world, completely detached from the physical organism. All this strengthened him enormously.

Third, he experienced the living presence of the Christ, crucified and risen. While always deeply Christian in his bones, during his years of philosophical preparation, when he had to discover the spirit out of his own resources, Steiner had often given the impression of having abandoned his Christian roots for a kind of spiritual free-thinking individualism, in which all religion, including the Christ, was a misperception of the human "I." Approaching his fortieth year, however, he was tested, with a purpose. As he says, "Tests of this nature are obstacles placed in one's path by destiny and have to be overcome in the course of spiritual development." The test involved truth and falsity. Since error on Earth is a spiritual being in the heavens, Steiner recognized that his struggle was with *Ahriman,* the principle of evil having to do with "premature" materialism and abstraction without full spiritual incarnation. The antidote, he realized intuitively, was "to contemplate the evolution of Christianity with spiritual perception." Doing so, he was led to the dawning of a new "conscious knowledge of true Christianity."

Around the turn of the century, this knowledge grew deeper. The inner test of soul, mentioned above, occurred shortly before the turn of the century. *This experience culminated in my standing spiritually in the presence of the Mystery of Golgotha in a most inward, profound, and solemn festival of knowledge.*

This was not a sudden illumination in which the whole meaning and experience of Christ's deed was revealed in its fullness all at once. Rather, it marked the beginning of a gradual process, which would continue to unfold for the rest of his life. Thus, only a few years later, after having written his first "Christian" texts, he could note: "1903—The Christian mysteries begin to dawn." As a spiritual researcher, an experimentalist, Steiner could never allow himself to know more than he could experience; and the path of experience, as anyone who follows it knows, is a continuous raising of the veils, which, while not a course of trial and error, is not one of complete knowledge, but of endless approach, forever drawing closer and deeper to reality, which is unknowable in its totality.

15

With the turn of the century, Rudolf Steiner began his spiritual teaching. Over the winter 1899–1900, in response to an invitation to address members of the German Theosophical Society, he gave a first series of lectures on mysticism and contemporary philosophy. Marie von Sivers (later, Marie Steiner) was one of those in attendance and immediately recognized him as the great teacher he was. Her contribution to world evolution is therefore inestimable. From that point on, she became Steiner's helpmeet and organizer. It is not clear whether without her he could have accomplished what he did.

The theme of his lectures was mysticism as a way of knowing: that is, *Know thyself*, in the large sense of "know yourself as an organ of divine-spiritual-cosmic cognition." The key was "Die and become" (Goethe) and "Those who do not die before they die, when they die, rot" (Jakob Böhme). To truly exist, then, to become an "I," one must sacrifice one's separate existence as determined by one's organic, psychological circumstances. This is the transformation that the injunction of the Delphic oracle requires. It does not ask us to know ourselves as psychological beings. In fact, the individual, separate personality must die for the Self to come into the world, the true Light, whose illumination allows us to see things as they are.

The following year, he spoke on Christianity as mystical fact. In book form, these two sets of lectures, *Mystics After Modernism* (or *Mysticism at the Dawn of the Modern Age*) and *Christianity As Mystical Fact,* exemplify what Steiner's approach to Theosophy would be.

He would take the Western path as it led from the religions of Persia and Egypt, through the ancient Greek philosophers and Mystery religions, into the Middle Ages of mysticism (Meister Eckhart, Nicholas of Cusa, Silesius), alchemy (Paracelsus, Basil Valentine, Böhme), and the beginnings of Freemasonry and Rosicrucianism, all the way up to Romanticism and German "Idealism" as indigenous Western European precursors of Theosophy.

He would bring Christ into Theosophy, making his entire vision and method pivot upon the "deed of Christ," Christ's presence in evolution, human nature, and the Earth, which he called "The Mystery of Golgotha."

16

The die was cast. On October 20, 1902, Rudolf Steiner became General Secretary of the German Theosophical Society with the proviso that he would teach only what he saw fit, that is, what he could vouch for from his own personal experience. Esoteric work began immediately on (at least) five fronts.

FIRST, the "sacred" literature of Theosophy had to be absorbed, sifted, and meditated through. However difficult it was for him to do so, Steiner worked through *Isis Unveiled* and *The Secret*

Doctrine, as well as Blavatsky's other works, including *The Voice of the Silence* and many essays and occasional pieces. Here his main intent was to make esotericism and its symbolism publicly available: to dissolve the distinction between exoteric and esoteric (that is, to ensure that the veil of the Temple was truly "rent"). He also spent time meditating Theosophical writers like Mabel Collins, whose work, especially *Light on the Path*, he held in high regard as an essential meditative text. He also undertook the direction of the Esoteric Section, whose purpose was to nurture the practical, not theoretical, pursuit of spiritual wisdom. He saw this enterprise as critical, for, as he wrote to Marie von Sivers (April, 1903):

> Often the people facing us are hardly with us at all because they are under the control of forces that lead them this way and that into life's trivialities and gradually become the nerve center of their lives. Such things can only be opposed by true and complete Theosophists.... *Without a nucleus of true Theosophists to improve the karma of the present by hard-working meditation, Theosophical teachings would be expounded merely to half-deaf ears.*

SECOND, the art of meditation had to be deepened from the bottom up. This meant beginning again (and again) the work of self-transformation, of dying to self. In this regard, a letter from Marie von Sivers (two days later), which shows her in a very human light, is revelatory:

> Today, for the first time, it seemed to me as if I understood the nature of meditation on a somewhat deeper level, which is more creative than reflection, re-petition, and re-feeling. I wanted to preserve it, but then my morning work intervened, and now the letters, and I fear it is disappearing. You will probably say that I should have preserved it, despite the interruptions. But in that situation, the absorbed peace of soul—a fundamental condition—is lost, because of things that have remained undone.

There you have my freshly acquired insight. That, by the way, was something I realized particularly clearly while meditating today. The main obstacle for me was disorder. It gave me a heightened feeling of being in a rush and of a guilty conscience. Thus things that had not been done and had been omitted in everyday life intruded into the devotional and mental images. This is a deeper reason for my slow progress and, as long as this vice is not pulled out by the roots, things will not go well. *One has to start with the small things.*

Meditation work is thus always also work on oneself. Work on oneself and the concomitant awareness of one's weaknesses and failings, however, should never be allowed to overwhelm or distract one from the fundamental path of the meditation itself, which is both teacher and teaching. If you persevere, it will do its work, irrespective of your distractions. If you are distracted, return to the the meditation. Meditation with themes and exercises that are elaborated and perfected from time immemorial by the great sages, teachers, mystics, and initiates will, by the grace of the spiritual world, change and instruct you. Only do it, start now: Do it for the sake of the world.

Hence, the THIRD point. The framework and ambiance of Steiner's meditation was *research.* The term is at once accurate and misleading. It is accurate to the extent that a constant product of the inner work he practiced and taught was *cognitive* and produced experiences of knowing or insight in relation to whatever field he was investigating. Yet, such investigation or research is rewarded by the spiritual world only when it is not undertaken for selfish purposes, but to advance human-Earthly evolution, that is, out of a sense of service and dedication. *Spiritual research is therefore a special kind of cognitive service.*

Initially at least, Steiner practiced research/meditation in four different areas. Theosophy was a vast compendium or reservoir of primordial esoteric symbols, doctrines, and teachings, often ill-digested, and at best half understood. One task was to penetrate these so profoundly as to be able to communicate and clothe them in a form and language accessible to contemporary consciousness. Another task was to penetrate the reality of evolution, under whose sign the Earth (and humanity) stood. Here Steiner walked a middle path between the abstract theories of Theosophy and the materialist literalism (nominalism) of modern evolutionary science. Following his old master Goethe, Steiner found this path by absorbing the wisdom of those he would later call the "old philosophers of nature," the alchemists. A third task was to revive and give new life to the moribund traditions of the West: Christian, Manichaean, Gnostic, Cathar, Grail, Rosicrucian, Masonic, and even Magic. Lastly, there was the continuous work of discovery with, for, and on the *Christ*. In all these endeavors, Steiner placed his work under the aegis of the Archangel Michael, Regent of our Age.

FOURTH, Steiner felt the need to connect, to assure continuity, with the representatives of the Western spiritual traditions, however decadent they might be. Anthroposophy was certainly something brand new, but it was equally something ancient, a heritage, with a lineage and ancestors that reached back through the ancient Mystery religions to the primordial teachers of humanity. Establishing connection meant spiritual, living union with this tradition through meditation and Earthly connection by actual transmission from existing representatives of different streams which, however decadent they might appear to be, nevertheless constituted the vehicle that assured continuity. "In order to preserve the continuity of human evolution it is necessary today to link up, as it were, with ritual and symbolism" (December 20, 1918). It is in this sense that we must understand the Rosicrucian, Masonic, Grail, and other initiatory elements that echo throughout Steiner's life and esoteric instructions collected here.

FIFTH, Steiner understood that if there is to be a true spiritual renewal that would break down the barriers between the exoteric and esoteric, the whole of life must become *sacramental*. What formerly took place only at the altar must be the prerogative of all humanity. This means that our whole life must become (in a cognitive sense) ritualized.

During this first period of spiritual teaching, besides giving countless lectures and holding esoteric meetings wherever he went (and building up a large body of spiritual students), Steiner wrote the basic texts of Anthroposophy: *How to Know Higher Worlds*, *Theosophy*, and *An Outline of Esoteric Science*. These, together with *The Philosophy of Freedom* (*Intuitive Thinking as a Spiritual Path*), constitute the core teaching.

The esoteric work was carried out under the auspices of the Esoteric Section and the Cognitive Cultic (Ritual) Section of the German Theosophical Society. As in Freemasonry, there were three Grades: Apprentice, Journeyman, and Master. There were also individual students, who worked with Steiner one-on-one. At the end of his life, when he instituted the so-called First Class (of the High School of Spiritual Science) it, too, was to be the first of three.

Esoteric work runs throughout Steiner's life, ceasing (apparently) only during the period of the Great War (1914–1918), though of course he continued to give private instruction and meditations during this period too. Outwardly, his focus shifted as his "research interests" moved: through Christ and the arts (1907–1914), to recognizing and overcoming evil (1914–1918), and into social action (1918–1922). The break with Theosophy came in 1913. The last years (1923–1925), following the burning of the first Goetheanum and the foundation of the General Anthroposophical Society until Steiner's death in 1925, were a true flowering. Anthroposophy, the new spiritual dispensation, shedding the jargon of outmoded occultism, entered ordinary language. The ancient Mysteries were open to all once again.

17

This collection contains texts for meditation that are representative of Steiner's spiritual method, philosophy, and practice. It contains nothing that does not emerge from his own experience and was not practiced by him, if not exactly in the form presented here, then in some very similar form.

The organization is self-explanatory. It begins with three short pieces that illuminate the framework within which anthroposophical work takes place. Basic meditation instructions and explanations follow. Next, a selection of meditation sentences illustrative of "the way of thinking," drawn predominantly from Steiner's key work *The Philosophy of Freedom (Intuitive Thinking as a Spiritual Path)* makes clear the cognitive foundations of the path. "The way of reverence" unfolds this path from its foundation in a certain soul mood and demonstrates how "devotion," "becoming as little children," can lead to transformations in our thinking, perceiving, feeling, and willing. This section is drawn from Steiner's classic *How to Know Higher Worlds*. Then come two basic practices: the so-called "six supplementary exercises" and the "backward review." This is followed by a manifold series of meditations for living the year spiritually. This anthroposophical "Book of Hours" contains, among others, the *Calendar of the Soul* verses, the verses for the days of the week, and the zodiac verses, as well as meditations for the different festivals. At the heart of the book are three sections drawn from Steiner's more explicitly esoteric work. This is followed by a selection of meditations for the dead. The book concludes with the central Foundation Stone meditation, which all who meditate following Rudolf Steiner should lay in their hearts. Finally, as a coda, the descriptions of meeting with the lesser and greater guardians of the threshold are presented. Therewith, readers in some sense are on their own in the company of the spiritual world.

There are, of course, many more practices than included here. The collection is by no means encyclopedic. Certain things have been left out entirely: for instance, karma and reincarnation research. Hopefully, however, enough has been given for those who wish to go deeper and further, to do so.

18

It is the essence of Rudolf Steiner's spiritual teaching that the student is free. Steiner does not wish to impose on our freedom. We shall choose our spiritual vocation (or it will choose us), according to our destiny and karma, which is our personal affair, and will come to us as a question of taste, style, aesthetics. We will create our own "beauty way." Steiner's own path, and what he hoped would be part of ours too, was lived under the sign of the Archangel Michael, the Regent of our Age, and in the service of Christ. He summarizes this path most movingly (and mysteriously) in his last lecture, given on Michaelmas Eve, 1924. He speaks of the sequence of incarnations of the being who was John the Baptist, the painter Raphael, and the inspired Romantic magic idealist, poet, philosopher, and novelist Novalis.

In Novalis, he says, we see "a radiant forerunner" of that Michael stream, which is "*to prepare the work to be accomplished at the end of the [twentieth] century and lead humanity through the great crisis in which it is involved.*"

Steiner then describes the work in the following way:

— Only when this work, which is to let the Michaelic power and will (which are only those that go before Christ's power and will to plant them in the Earth in the right way) penetrate the whole of life;

— Only when Michael's power can truly conquer all that is demonic and dragon-like (you well know what that is);

— Only when all of you have received this Michaelic thought with true and faithful heart and inward love; and endeavor to go forward until not only is Michael's thought *revealed in your soul,* but you are also able to make this Michael thought *live in your deeds* in all its strength and power;

— Only then will you be *true servants* of the Michael thought, *worthy helpers* of what must now enter world evolution as Michael intends it through Anthroposophy....

He goes on:

This is what I would have my words today speak to your soul:

that you receive this Michael thought as a heart faithful to Michael may feel when Michael appears clothed in the light rays of the Sun and points to what must happen for this Michael garment, this garment of light, to become the Cosmic Words that are Christ's Words that are Cosmic Words that can transform the Cosmic Logos into the Human Logos.

Then Steiner speaks his last public words:

Springing from the powers of the Sun,
You, shining, world-blessing spirit powers:
Divine thinking predestined you
To be Michael's coat of rays.

Christ's messenger, he reveals in you,
Bearers of humanity, the holy will of worlds;
You, bright beings of the ether worlds,
Bear Christ's word to humankind.

Thus the herald of the Christ appears
To waiting, thirsting souls;
To them your word of light streams forth
In the cosmic age of spirit humans.
You, students of spirit knowledge
Take Michael's wise gesture,
Take into your soul's high purpose
The word of love of the will of worlds.

19

Every text is an occasion to encounter its author. This is especially true of spiritual writings. Reading the words of a St. Francis or a Jacob Böhme, we feel we have entered the presence of and are face-to-face with a great soul, whose dedication and intimacy with the divine has allowed the spiritual world to communicate itself through it. In this sense every work of Rudolf Steiner's is a portrait of him and of his relationship to the spirit. Every work is a gateway to meeting Rudolf Steiner and through him, the spiritual world. The more intimate the work, the more this is true. And nothing is more intimate than these meditation texts, many of which in fact were given to specific individuals. These texts allow us to meet Rudolf Steiner as teacher—the rest is up to us.

Prologue—Framing the Work

Meditation is certainly above all a matter of attention or heightened conscious awareness. It is equally and naturally a question of method. It makes a difference, for instance, whether one starts with the breath, the bodily posture, or thinking. The frame within which one situates one's meditation, however, also makes a difference. Ideally, perhaps, as Krishnamurti famously insisted, there would be neither method nor frame, but only pure attention. For most of us, however, that is impossible. We are situated; we seek to explore the world from a certain perspective; and so we meditate in a tradition with its own understanding of the world. The following short selection seeks to give some idea of the framework of anthropsophical meditation taught by Rudolf Steiner.

1. Credo: The Individual and the All

The following short, programmatic text contains many sentences that can be meditated. It articulates the principles of the path of Anthroposophy and the anthroposophical worldview that Steiner was to follow for half a century. First discovered only in 1944, and covering three handwritten, undated sheets, it probably dates from 1888. Steiner was then twenty-seven years old and deeply immersed in the study of Goethe.

The world of ideas is the primal source and principle of all being. Endless harmony and blessed rest are contained within it. Being, unillumined by its light, would be a dead thing, without essence. It would play no part in the life of the world totality. Only what derives existence from the Idea means something on the tree of universal creation. The Idea is Spirit—clear and sufficient in and unto itself. Whatever is singular, particular, and individual must find the Spirit in itself. If it does not, it will fall from the tree of the universe like a dead leaf and will have existed in vain.

Human beings feel and know themselves as individuals when they awake to full consciousness. So that we might awake, yearning for the Idea is planted in us. This yearning leads us to overcome our particularity. It allows Spirit to live in us and allows us to conform ourselves to the Spirit. In and from ourselves, we must rise up and cast off all that is selfish, all that makes us this particular, individual being. For this particularity is what darkens the light of the Spirit. All that we do out of sensuality, instinct, lust, and passion serves only the egotistic individual. We must kill this self-seeking will in ourselves. As individuals, we must will what the Spirit, the Idea, wills in us. Let particularity go, follow the voice of the Idea in you, for that alone is divine!

To will as a separate being is to be a worthless point at the periphery of the universe, disappearing in the stream of time. To will "in the Spirit" is to be at the center, for then the central light of the universe resurrects in you. If you act as a separate being you lock yourself out of the closed chain of world action. You cut yourself out. If you act in the Spirit, you live into universal world action. The killing of all *selfness* is the foundation for a higher life. For whoever destroys selfness lives in eternal being. To the extent that we have let selfness die in us, we are immortal. Selfness is what is mortal in us. This is the true meaning of the saying, "If you don't die before you die, when you die, you rot." That is, those who do not allow egotism to cease during the time of their earthly life have no part in the universal life that is immortal. Such a person never really existed, had no true being.

There are four spheres of human activity in which we can dedicate ourselves to the Spirit by killing all selfish life. These are the spheres of knowledge, art, religion, and the loving, spiritual dedication to a person. Whoever does not live in at least one of these four spheres does not live at all. Knowledge is dedication to the universal in thought; art is dedication to the universal in contemplation; religion is dedication to the universal in feeling; and love is dedication—with all our spiritual forces—to something that seems to us to be an invaluable being in the world totality. Knowledge is the most spiritual form of selfless dedication, and love is the most beautiful. Love is the true light of heaven in everyday life. Love ennobles our being right into its innermost fiber. It lifts all that lives in us. Pure, devout love transforms our whole soul life into another life that has a relationship with the world Spirit. In this highest sense, to love means to bear the breath of divine life where mostly shameful egotism and careless passion are to be found. Before we may speak of devotion, we must know something of the holiness of love.

Those who have passed out of separateness and lived through one of these four spheres and into divine life have reached the goal for which the seed of yearning was placed in their hearts—union with the Spirit. This is a true definition. Those who live in the spirit, live free; they have freed themselves from all secondary things. Nothing compels them, other than that by which they are gladly compelled, for they have known it as the highest.

Let truth come to life. Lose yourself in order to find yourself again in the world Spirit.

2. *Ideas are to Thinking as Light is to the Eye*

In the following paragraph from Steiner's introductory essay on Goethe's theory of knowledge, published around the same time as the Credo was written, every sentence is packed with significance and implications. It is perhaps not too far-fetched to say that starting from these few lines one could generate much of Anthroposophy.

The objects of thinking are ideas. When our thinking comprehends an idea, it unites with the foundations of universal existence. What is actively at work in the outer world enters the human spirit. The human being unites with objective reality in its highest potency. *Beholding the idea in outer reality is the true communion of humanity.* Thinking relates to ideas as the eye relates to light and the ear to sound; it is an organ of perception.

3. Dialog of Master and Student

This dialog was written by Rudolf Steiner in a notebook around 1908. It was probably the fruit of his own meditative practice and research, as well as something that he taught his pupils in the Esoteric School. Read carefully; it has much to teach us about how to understand the process of meditation and avoid the various pitfalls of egotism.

Student: What is the way to life in the suprasensory worlds, where spirits create and souls cognize?

Master: When you can succeed in existing for a while where no dependent beings touch you, you will stand in the spirits' creating. If you can succeed in existing for a while where no sense perceptions speak to you, then you will cognize through the soul's power.

Student: Where is the place to which you are directing me?

Master: The place is in the "I," but you will find it only when you abandon your "I," when *your* will is silent and *your* senses extinguished, and you say "I will" and in a living way, "I think."

Student: How can I become capable of saying "I will" when my will is silent? How can I become capable of animating the "I think" when my senses are extinguished?

Master: Only willing that you do not will manifests the "I." Only the thought that you do not think kindles the "spirit."

—Notebook Archive no. 488 (GA 226/I)

4. Two Leading Thoughts

Starting in February 1924 and continuing until his death in March 1925, Rudolf Steiner wrote a series of articles in the Newsletter for Members of the newly formed General Anthroposophical Society. Each article concluded with a number of so-called leading thoughts, or "guiding principles." These principles are a summation of Steiner's work and reaching. I include the first and the last (written just before he died and published two weeks later).

FIRST LEADING THOUGHT

Anthroposophy is a path of knowledge, a cognitive path, seeking to lead what is spiritual in human beings to what is spiritual in the universe. It comes to human beings as a need of the heart and the feelings, and is justified only insofar as it satisfies this need. Those people recognize Anthroposophy who find in it what they themselves are impelled to seek out of their souls' inner core. Hence only those can be Anthroposophists who experience certain questions about human nature and the universe as a vital necessity like hunger and thirst.

PENULTIMATE LEADING THOUGHT

During the age of natural science, which began about the middle of the nineteenth century, human cultural activity has slipped gradually not just into the lowest realms of nature, but actually *under nature*. Technology becomes *Sub-Nature*.

This requires that human beings now experience a knowledge of the spirit in which they raise themselves into *Supra-Nature*. They must raise themselves as high above nature as they sink down below nature in sub-natural technological activity. By this means, they create inwardly the strength *not to go under*.

Meditation Instructions and Explanations

Rudolf Steiner was remarkably consistent and simple in the instructions and explanations he gave on meditation. What he said remained more or less the same throughout the twenty years or so that he functioned as an esoteric teacher.

Set aside a brief period every day

Here the basics are established. We enter as deeply within ourselves as we can. Sense impressions, memories, associations, thoughts, hopes and dreams, all fade away. In the inner silence, peace descends upon the soul. It becomes receptive, opening to and receiving what the spirit gives. This can happen without a theme, but, as Steiner suggests, concentrating on a theme of eternal wisdom to the exclusion of all other thoughts is perhaps the easier way.

We must set aside a brief period every day for meditation. Whatever short time we can take—without conflicting with our responsibilities—is sufficient, even if it is only five minutes or less daily. During this time, we must be able to tear ourselves away from everything our sense impressions offer us—everything we take in through our eyes, ears, and sense of touch. We must become blind and deaf to our surroundings. All that approaches us from outside links us to the sensory world, to everyday life. All that must fall silent for a while. Complete inner peace must descend.

Once we accomplish this inner peace—this stripping off of all sensory impressions—we must also silence all recollection of past sensory impressions. Just think how all I have just listed binds us to time and space and to all that comes into being and passes away. Try testing this. Check the thought that was going through your head a minute ago—was it related to something transitory? Such thoughts are not suited to inner development. All thoughts connecting us to the finite and transitory must fall silent.

When peace has been produced in the soul, when the time, race, nationality, and century we are embedded in have been overcome, and inner silence has descended for a time, then *the soul begins to speak of its own accord.*

This does not happen immediately. First, we must bring the soul to the point of speaking. There are ways and means of doing so.

One method is to submit to thoughts, images, and sensations that originate in eternity rather than in passing time. It is not enough that such thoughts or images were true a hundred years ago, or that they are true for today, yesterday, or tomorrow. *They must be true forever.* You will find such thoughts in the various religious books of all peoples—in the Bhagavad Gita (the Song of Human Perfection), for example, and in the New and Old Testaments, especially the Gospel of St. John from chapter thirteen on. Thoughts that are particularly effective for people who belong to the Theosophical movement are provided in Mabel Collins's book *Light on the Path*, especially in the first four sentences.

1. Before the eyes can see, they must be incapable of tears.

2. Before the ear can hear, it must have lost its sensitiveness.

3. Before the voice can speak in the presence of the Masters, it must have lost the power to wound.

4. Before the soul can stand in the presence of the Masters, its feet must be washed in the blood of the heart.

These four sentences, which are engraved on the interior walls of every temple of initiation, are independent of time and space. They do not belong to an individual, a family, a century, or a generation; they extend throughout evolution. They were true thousands of years ago and will be true for thousands of years to come. They awaken forces that sleep within us and draw them up.

This must be done in the right way. It is not enough to think that we understand such a sentence. We must let it come alive within us. We must submit to it totally, allowing all its power to radiate within us. We must learn to love the sentence. When we believe we have understood it, that simply means the time has come to allow it to shine within us again and again. Our intellectual understanding of the sentence is not the point; the point is to love its spiritual truth. The more we love such inner truths and feel this love streaming through us, the more the power of inner sight awakens in us. If we remain involved with such a sentence not only for a day or two but for weeks, months, and years, it will awaken soul forces within us. This is followed by another illumination at a very specific moment.

—Berlin, December 15, 1904

Early in the morning

The following instructions were given to an entering student of the Esoteric School, Anna Wagner. Interestingly, before he gives his instructions, Steiner mentions that the "Masters," or so-called Mahatmas, themselves stand behind the Esoteric School and guide it. The important implication is that, when we meditate, we should recognize that we do not do so alone, that spiritual beings accompany us and are present with us. We never meditate alone!

Early in the morning, before doing anything else, if possible even before breakfast (if that is compatible with family and other duties):

1. You should become completely awake, inwardly perfectly at peace and collected. Allow no outer impressions to enter you. Suppress all memories of everyday experience. Once you have established complete "inner stillness," pass into your higher Self. For this, concentrate your thoughts on the following formula for about five minutes:

> More radiant than the Sun,
> Purer than the Snow,
> Subtler than the Ether,
> Is the Self,
> The Spirit within my heart.
> I am that Self,
> That Self am I.

2. Then reflect in silent absorption for another five minutes on a sentence from an inspired text. For instance, during this part of the meditation, immerse yourself reflectively in the sentence:

> Steadfastness stands higher than any success.

3. Then, after five minutes on that sentence, spend a final five minutes in prayer-like surrender (dedication and reverence) oriented to whatever is highest or most divine for you. This is not a matter of regarding this or that as divine, but of turning all your thoughts and feelings and your whole will to whatever you have always regarded as divine. Some people will call this one thing, some another. It makes no difference whether you call what you surrender to God, Christ, or "the Master." What is important is the mood of surrender (devotion) itself.

With this, the threefold morning meditation, which lasted about fifteen minutes, is finished.

Do your meditation as well as possible

Here Rudolf Steiner gives encouragement to Marie von Sivers, his coworker, who would become his wife, on the importance of continually striving and the (relative) unimportance of how successful we are.

Do your meditation as well as possible. After all, the light that falls on the intellectual grasp of esoteric things has its source there. Even if you do not notice it, the meditations and concentration exercises that you now have contain the key to much. They have been formulated from ancient times by the great adepts and if you patiently bring them to life in your soul, you will gain the truth of seven worlds from them. They contain the secrets of the initiates. And those who know how to use them correctly have the possibility of shedding the three forms of lower worlds and of maturing gradually even to the state of the Swan. *You must not worry about imperfections in meditating. But always strive to do the best that lies in your power.*

—Letter to Marie von Sivers, April 11, 1905

Rhythm, or regularity

Night follows day, the Earth turns about the Sun, the seasons unfold one into the other with fidelity and constancy. Rhythm, with its repetition, always lies at the heart of spiritual life, as it does of all life. The "canonical hours" of monastic practice immediately come to mind. But we do not need to live in a monastery to experience the mysteries of rhythm.

It is more necessary today than it was in earlier times for human beings to bring rhythm into all spheres of higher life. Just as rhythm is implanted in the physical body by God, so we must give our astral bodies rhythm. We must order our day for ourselves. We must arrange the rhythm of our day for the astral body, just as the spirit of nature arranges it for the lower realms.

In the morning, at a definite time, you must undertake one spiritual action; a different one must be undertaken at another time, again to be performed regularly, and yet another in the evening. These spiritual exercises must not be chosen arbitrarily, but should be suitable for the development of higher life. This is one method for taking hold of life and for keeping hold of it.

Set a time for yourself in the morning when you can *concentrate.* Stick to this time. Establish a kind of calm so that the esoteric master in you may awaken. You must *meditate* on a great thought that has nothing to do with the outer world. Let this thought content come to life completely within you. A short time will suffice for this, perhaps a quarter of an hour. Even five minutes are enough if more time is not available. *It is worthless to do these exercises irregularly.* You must do them regularly so that the activity of the astral body becomes regular as a clock. Only then do they have value.

If you do these exercises regularly, the astral body will appear completely different. Sit down in the morning and do these exercises, and the forces I have described will develop. But, as I said, you must do this *regularly,* for the astral body expects that the same process will take place at the same time each day, and it falls into disorder if this does not happen. At least, the intent toward order must exist. If you give your life a rhythm in this way, you will see success before long; in other words, the spiritual life hidden from you for now will manifest to a certain degree.

—Berlin, December 7, 1905

Meditation as soul exercise

The following description comes from a paper Steiner delivered at a philosophy conference. It makes clear that meditation is also and always a way of knowing, a cognitive, "philosophical" activity.

What I am about to propose may be described as a "soul exercise." We begin by considering, *from another point of view,* certain contents of the soul that are usually taken as images or representations of some outer reality. In the concepts and ideas that we make for ourselves we usually try to find something that is an image or at least a sign of something *outside* the concepts or ideas. Spiritual researchers—in the sense meant here—also start with soul contents like the concepts and ideas of ordinary life or scientific research. But they do not consider their cognitive value in relation to something objective ["outside"]. Rather, *they let them live in their souls as an effective force.* They sink them, so to speak, as spiritual seeds into the mother ground of psychic life and wait in complete peace of soul for them to work upon their soul life. They can then observe how, by repeated practice of such an exercise, the condition of the soul actually changes. I must stress that everything depends upon repeating the exercise. It is not a question of the conceptual contents—in the ordinary sense—causing something like a cognitive process to occur in the soul. It has to do rather with a real process in soul life itself. In this process, the concepts do not work as cognitive elements, but as real forces. And their working depends upon these forces repeatedly taking hold of soul life. Above all, everything depends upon the fact that the work in the soul, which is achieved through experience with a concept, is repeatedly grasped with the same force. *The best results occur when the same meditation is practiced at repeated intervals over an extended period of time.* The actual length of the meditation has little to do with it. It can be very short if it is accomplished with absolute peace of soul, and with the complete exclusion of all sense impressions and ordinary mental activity. It all comes down to the isolation of one's soul life with a given content.

   This needs to be mentioned because it must be clearly understood that undertaking these soul exercises need not disturb anyone in their ordinary lives. The time required, as a rule, is available to everyone, and if the exercises are performed correctly, the change they bring about in the soul should not produce the slightest effect upon the constitution of consciousness necessary for normal life....

For these soul exercises, the ordinary concepts of life are for the most part unusable. All soul contents that relate to objective elements lying outside the soul work only minimally for these soul exercises.

Representations we can designate as *symbols* work much better. Most fruitful among these are those which draw together the greatest content in a living way. An example of such a symbol, proven by experience to be good, is what Goethe called "the archetypal plant."... Whatever one may think of the cognitive value of such a symbolic "archetypal plant," if it is made to live in the soul in the way I have indicated, and if one awaits with serenity its working in one's soul life, then something enters that one may call a different soul constitution.

The representations that spiritual researchers say may be used as symbols for this work may at times seem very strange.... [*Steiner goes on to mention appropriate kinds of symbols for meditation—a centaur (half human, half animal); the Caduceus, or Staff of Mercury; mathematical forms, such as the "Cassini curve"; and word meditations, such as "Wisdom lives in the Light."*]

—"The Psychological Foundations and Epistemological
Position of Anthroposophy," 1911

A useful analogy

There are two ways of knowing. In the first, which is ordinary consciousness or sense perception, the act of perceiving or thinking is immediately transformed or abstracted (frozen) into a representation or object; in the second, we try to avoid objectifying in favor of a continuous process of metamorphosis. The second is to "kiss the bird in flight and fly with it"; the first shoots it down.

Look at a few grains of wheat. They can be applied for the purposes of nutrition. Alternatively they can be planted in the soil, so that other wheat plants develop from them. The representations and ideas acquired through sensory experience can be retained in the mind with the effect that what is experienced in them is a reproduction of sensory reality. But they can also be experienced in another way: The energy they evince in the psyche by virtue of what they are, quite apart from the fact that they reproduce phenomena, can be allowed to act itself out. The first way may be compared to what happens to the wheat grains when a living creature assimilates them as its means of nourishment. The second may be compared to engendering a new wheat plant through each grain. Of course, we must bear in mind that what is produced is a plant similar to its parent, whereas the outcome from an idea active in the mind is a force available for the formation of organs of the spirit. It must also be borne in mind that initial awareness of such inner forces can be kindled only by particularly potent ideas ... but once the mind has been alerted to the presence of such forces, other ideas and representations may also serve, though not quite so well, for further progress in the direction it has now taken.

—"Anthropology and Anthroposophy,"
from *The Riddle of the Soul*, 1917

What is essential?

In this late lecture, Steiner stresses the fundamental aspect of all spiritual practice: attention.

I would like to draw your attention to how meditation is done in its simplest form. I can deal only with basic principles today. This is what we are dealing with: An idea, or image, or combination thereof, is moved to the center of our consciousness....

What is essential? Everything depends on gathering our whole soul life upon the content of the meditation. Just as the muscles of the arm become strong as we work with them, we strengthen our soul forces by repeatedly focusing them on the meditative content. If possible, the content of meditation should remain the same for months or even years. For genuine spiritual research the forces of the soul must first be strengthened and empowered.

If we continue practicing in this way, the day will come, I would like to say, the big day, when we make a very special observation. Gradually we notice that we are in a soul activity entirely independent of the body.

—London, August 20, 1922

Requirements

What does it take to be an esoteric student? The following words from one of Steiner's esoteric lessons make it clear.

Five requirements are asked of the student:

1. Purgation of the heart
2. Purification of love
3. Emptiness of memory
4. Clarity of understanding
5. Extinguishing or kindling of the will

The heart must be purged. Love must lose all unchaste qualities and become divine. Memory, to become objective, must not hold onto anything that could awaken preconceptions, prejudices. The understanding must be clear and the will, where it is selfish, must be extinguished; but where it serves as the toll of the master, it must be kindled.

—December 28, 1905

Patience

Lest we forget, Steiner here makes clear the cardinal virtue.

The student should always bear in mind the foundational statement:

I can wait patiently.

Impatient striving (effort) does nothing to advance us. Whatever one does will bear fruit in the future.

Four dangers that must be mastered and overcome

The path is never without its dangers. Once again, Steiner sums them up clearly and concisely.

There are four dangers that must be mastered and overcome:

I. The materialist danger, which lives in the physical body, or is the physical body
2. The clairvoyant danger, whose seat is the ether body
3. The magical danger, which the astral body brings
4. The mystical danger, which is the "I"

The materialist danger is when the lower self closes off access to the above; then egotism increases all the more.

The clairvoyant danger is when one draws down the higher worlds. If one draws down the higher worlds, one can become worse through the exercises.

The magical danger manifests when it is believed that one is receiving orders and so on. We never hear commands from higher beings. They never say, "You must!"

The mystical danger is when we confuse our own desires with what comes from above.

—September 1908

The Way of Thinking

"To lay hold of thinking in oneself is to lay hold on the Divine."
—Rudolf Steiner, *Mystery Knowledge and Mystery Centers*

"Thinking" is the heart and blood of what distinguishes Steiner's approach to spiritual work. The thinking that he is talking about, however, is not our ordinary thinking by which we rearrange existing (past, dead) thoughts. By thinking Steiner means "living" thinking, the dynamic process-state before thinking becomes thoughts. It is, as it were, "thinking without an object," which, in some sense, could also be a definition of attention.

Trust in thinking

Trust allows us to live in the stream of thinking, which is the first stage of meditation. According to Steiner, "The soul naturally trusts in thinking." We must cultivate this trust. When we do so and we live in the stream of thinking, it is as if cosmic existence were flowing through us. We realize that "the world thinks itself in the human soul." As he puts it in *A Way of Self-Knowledge*:

For everyday, awake consciousness, human thinking is an island in the river of soul life that flows by in impressions, sensations, feelings, and so on. Once we have understood a feeling or impression—that is, once we have created a thought to illuminate it—we are more or less finished with it. Even amid a storm of passions and emotions, a certain calm arises when the barque of the soul reaches the island of thought.

The soul trusts naturally in thinking. Were it to lose this trust in thinking, the soul would lose all certainty in life. Once we begin to doubt thinking, healthy soul life stops. Even if thinking cannot always bring us clarity about something, at least we need the comfort of knowing that we *could* attain that clarity if only we were able to summon sufficient mental strength and sharpness. A person can come to terms with being unable to bring clarity to something through thinking, but the idea that thinking itself could not bring satisfaction—even if one were to push as deeply into it as should be necessary to attain the complete clarity required by a particular situation—that idea is unbearable.

This attitude of the soul toward thinking lies at the heart of all human striving for knowledge. Certain states of mind can dampen it. Nevertheless, in its own dark depths, the soul always feels it can think. Thinkers who doubt the validity and power of thinking deceive themselves about the basic tone of their souls. Often it is the very sharpness of their thought that, by a kind of excess, creates their doubts and perplexities. If they really did not trust thinking, they would not torture themselves so much with doubts and riddles, which are themselves only the results of thinking.

If you develop this feeling of trust in relation to thinking, you will find that thinking contains not only something that you form inwardly as the power of the human soul, but also a power that is independent of both you and your soul and that bears within it a cosmic being—toward whom you must work if you wish to inhabit a place that belongs simultaneously both to you and to the world that is independent of you.

There is something deeply calming in being able to surrender oneself to the life of thought. In it, the soul feels it can get away from itself. The soul needs this feeling just as much as it needs the opposite feeling—that of being able to be totally within itself. Oscillation between these two is necessary for a healthy soul life. Wakefulness and sleep are only the extreme manifestations of this oscillation. In wakefulness, the soul is in itself; it lives its own life. In sleep, the soul loses itself in universal cosmic experience and is, in a sense, free of itself. We can also see these two extremes of the pendulum-like movement of the soul in other states of inner experience. Living in one's thoughts, for example, is an instance of the soul's getting away from itself, whereas living in feeling, sensation, emotion, and so forth, are all instances of the soul's dwelling in itself.

From this perspective, thinking gives the soul the consolation it needs in the face of feeling abandoned by the world. You are certainly justified in wondering, *What am I in the general stream of world events that runs from infinity to infinity? What am I with my feelings, wishes, and deeds, which have meaning only for me?* As soon as you have truly felt what it is to live in thought, you will be able to counter this feeling of abandonment with another perspective: *The thinking involved in this stream of world events raises me up, and my soul with me, and I live in those events when I allow their essence to flow into me through my thinking.* Thus, you can feel yourself taken up into the world and feel legitimate within it. This attitude of the soul results in a kind of strengthening, which the soul experiences as deriving according to wise laws from cosmic powers.

It is not a great leap from this perspective to one that says, *It is not merely I who think, for it thinks in me — world-becoming expresses itself in me and my soul provides only the stage upon which the world lives as thought.*

Philosophies can, of course, reject this attitude. There are many grounds on which the idea that "the world thinks itself in the human soul" can be made to seem obviously false. We must recognize, however, that this is an idea that can be acquired only through inner experience. Only those who have acquired it in this way can fully understand its validity. They know that so-called refutations cannot shake that validity. Anyone who has thought his or her way through this thought can see quite clearly the real value of most so-called refutations and proofs which, as long as one remains falsely convinced of their content, often appear quite infallible. Thus, it is difficult to communicate with those who find such counterproofs convincing. They have no choice but to believe in them, for they have not done the inner work required to understand the inner experience that brought the other person to the recognition they think is false or, perhaps, simply foolish.

Anyone wishing to become familiar with the practice of spiritual science will find such meditations on thinking useful. The work of this kind of meditation is to bring the soul to a state that opens a doorway into the spiritual world. That doorway will remain closed, no matter how ingenious the thinking or how fully scientific the approach, unless the soul prepares to advance to meet the approaching spiritual experiences (or, indeed, even the account of them).

A good preparation for understanding spiritual insights is to feel frequently what strength lies in the mood or attitude of soul when one meditates the thought: *In thinking, I experience myself united with the stream of cosmic existence.*

The value of meditating this thought lies much less in the abstract understanding of it than in what is to be gained by repeatedly experiencing the strengthening effect it has on the soul if it flows powerfully through one's inner life. It expands in the soul like a deep spiritual breath of life. Far more than cognizing the content of such a thought, it is *experiencing* it that is important. Let the thought be present only *once* in your soul with sufficient conviction, and you can understand it. But if it is to bear fruit in the understanding of the beings and facts of the spiritual world, then, when you have understood it, you must repeatedly bring it to life again in your soul. Again and again, you must fill your soul with the same thought. Only that thought must fill your soul, excluding all other thoughts, feelings, and memories.

Repeatedly concentrating on a thought that one has completely penetrated gathers the forces of the soul—forces that in normal life are scattered. The soul strengthens itself—in itself—and the powers that have been gathered together become organs of perception for the spiritual world and its truths.

This brief description indicates the right way to proceed in meditation. First, you work your way through to grasping a thought that you can fully understand with the means provided by everyday life and ordinary thinking. Then you sink yourself repeatedly into that thought, become absorbed in it, and make yourself wholly one with it. By living with a thought known in this way, your soul gains strength.

Above, a thought about the nature of thinking itself was chosen as an example, because it is particularly fruitful for meditation. But what was said about meditation applies to every thought that we thoroughly penetrate.

It is especially fruitful for a meditator to know the mood of soul that results from the pendulum-like movement of soul life as described above. It is the surest way to come to the feeling in your meditation that the spiritual world has touched you directly.

This feeling is a healthy consequence of meditation. It should radiate its strength into everything you do during the rest of your waking day. But it should not be a continuous, ever-present prolongation of the meditative state. Rather, you should feel, *Strength flows into my life from my meditation experience.*

If you carry your meditative state into daily life like an ever-present imprint, something will spread from it that will disturb the natural simplicity of your daily life. Then, during the meditation itself, your meditative state will no longer be either strong or pure enough. The true fruits of meditation are brought to maturity only when we raise our meditation and meditative state above the rest of our life. Meditation will have the best effect upon our lives when we experience it to be something special, something uplifting.

Intuitive thinking and the path to freedom

Steiner was thirty-three when *The Philosophy of Freedom* appeared in 1894. It had germinated in him for fourteen years. When it came to fruition, it was not so much the content that was important to him but its independent, existential value. As he wrote to his friend Rosa Mayreder with whom he had conversed at length as the book developed, Steiner mourned the fact that Nietzsche would never read his book, for he would have seen it for what it was: "personal experience in every sentence." Steiner goes on to say that his reasons for writing it were purely "subjective." He was not setting forth a doctrine, but simply recording inner experiences. He reported them as he experienced them. In other words, his purpose was "to write a biographical account of how one human soul made the difficult ascent to freedom." Obviously, to walk the path that Steiner walked, it is important to read and reread meditatively every word and sentence as he wrote it. To do so, as he himself states on many occasions, is a transformative experience and the basis for a real understanding of Anthroposophy. Precisely because of its fundamental importance, I have (perhaps to the chagrin and outrage of some) extracted certain key sentences and sets of sentences for meditation.

Steiner begins with the fundamental split that places us outside and against the world. Elsewhere, he writes, "The root of human imperfection lies in the division of primal unity into subject and object. In the realm of action, this imperfection takes the form of unfreedom. We are unfree in actions in which the interpenetration of subject and object has not taken place, and we are under the power of the object." Before we can overcome the split, however, we must first become aware of it.

THE SPLIT

What we seek in things, beyond what is immediately given to us, splits our entire being into two. We immediately become aware of standing in opposition to the world as independent beings. The universe appears to us as two opposites: I and the world.

We set up this barrier between ourselves and the world as soon as consciousness lights up within us. But we never lose the feeling that we belong to the world, that a link exists that connects us to it, and that we are creatures not outside but within the universe.

This feeling engenders an effort to bridge the opposition. And in the final analysis the whole spiritual striving of humanity consists in bridging this opposition. The history of spiritual life is a continual searching for the unity between I and the World.

The Way to Heal the Split

Only when we have made the world content into our thought content do we rediscover the connection from which we have sundered ourselves.

The Cause of the Split

It is we who separate ourselves from the native ground of nature and place ourselves as "I" in opposition to the world. Goethe gives this its classical expression: "We live in Nature's midst and are strangers to her."

Ariadne's Thread

To be sure, we have torn ourselves away from nature, but we must still have taken something of her with us into our own being.

The First Step

We can find nature outside us only if we first know her within us. What is akin to her within us will be our guide. We must seek out this natural being within ourselves; then we will also discover the reconnection to her.

The Two Points of Departure

Insofar as we are conscious of it, observation and thinking are the two points of departure for all human spiritual striving.... Philosophers have proceeded from various primal oppositions— such as idea and reality, subject and object, appearance and thing-in-itself, I and not I, idea and will, concept and matter, force and substance, conscious and unconscious—but it can easily be shown that observation and thinking precede all of these as the most important antithesis of human beings.

OBSERVING THINKING

Thinking differs essentially, as an object of observation, from all other things.... While observation of objects and processes, and thinking about them, are both everyday situations that fill my ongoing life, the observation of thinking is a kind of exceptional state....

When we observe thinking, we are applying to thinking a procedure—observation—that is normal when we consider all the rest of our world content, but that is not normally applied to thinking itself.

✸

This is the characteristic nature of thinking. The thinker forgets thinking while doing it.... It is the unobserved element in our normal spiritual life.

✸

It is because thinking is based on my own activity that I do not observe it in everyday life.

✸

When I think, I do not look at my thinking, which I myself am producing, but at the object of thinking, which I am not thinking.

I am in the same situation even if I allow the exceptional state of affairs to occur and think about my thinking. I can never observe my present thinking....

These two are therefore incompatible: active production and its objective confrontation.

A CORNER OF THE WORLD

In thinking we hold a corner of world process where we must be present if anything is to occur.

THE ESSENCE OF THINKING

We must not confuse having "thought pictures" with working out one's thoughts by means of thinking. Thought pictures emerge dreamily in the soul, like vague suggestions. But this is not thinking.... The essence of thinking always requires that it be willed.

☆

Unprejudiced observation shows that nothing can be attributed to the essence of thinking that is not found within thinking itself. One cannot arrive at anything that causes thinking if one leaves the realm of thinking behind.

WHERE CONCEPT AND OBSERVATION MEET

It is through the thinker that thinking is linked to observation. Human consciousness is the stage where concept and observation meet and are connected with each other. This is, in fact, what characterizes human consciousness. It is the mediator between thinking and observation.

SUBJECT AND OBJECT

We must not overlook the fact that it is only with the help of thinking that we can define ourselves as subjects, and contrast ourselves to objects. Therefore, thinking must never be regarded as a merely subjective activity. Thinking is beyond subject and object. It forms both of these concepts, as it does all others. Thus, when we, as thinking subjects, relate a concept to an object, we must not regard this relationship as merely subjective. It is not the subject that introduces the relationship but thinking. The subject does not think because it is a subject; rather, it appears to itself as a subject because it can think. The activity that human beings exercise as thinking beings is therefore not merely subjective, but it is a kind of activity that is neither subjective nor objective: it goes beyond both. I should never say that my individual subject thinks; rather, it lives by the grace of thinking.

THE MOVE TO THE CENTER

In thinking, we are given the element that unites our own particular individuality with the whole of the cosmos. When we sense, feel, and perceive, we are separate. When we think, we are the one being that penetrates all. This is the deeper basis of our dual nature. Within us, we see an absolute force come into existence that is universal. Yet we do not know it as it streams forth from the center of the world, but only at a point on the periphery. If we came to know it as it streamed forth from the center, then we would know the whole mystery of the world at the moment we became conscious. But we stand on the periphery, and find our existence enclosed within certain limits. Therefore, we must find out about the realm situated outside our own being with the help of thinking that extends into us from universal world existence.

CONCEPT AND PERCEPT TOGETHER MAKE THE WHOLE

For thinking beings, a concept arises from the encounter with an external thing. The concept is that part of the thing that we do not receive from without, but from within. Knowledge means to accomplish the union of the two elements, inner and outer.

A percept, then, is not something finished or closed off. It is one side of the total reality. The other side is the concept. The act of knowing (or cognition) is the synthesis of percept and concept. Only percept and concept make up the whole thing.

[Percept ... should not be confused with that of external sensory perception, which is only a particular case of it. Readers will see from what has been said, but still more so from what will be said later, that everything both sensory and spiritual that meets a human being is to be taken as percept until it is grasped by an actively elaborated concept.]

MERE PERCEPTION

Consider the world of percepts by itself. It appears as a mere juxta-position in space, a mere succession in time, and an aggregate of unconnected details. None of the things that enter or exit the per-ceptual stage seem to have anything to do with one another. In the world of percepts, the world is a multiplicity of uniform objects. None plays a greater role than any other.... If we are to have the insight that this or that has greater significance than another, we must consult our thinking.

INTUITION

In contrast to perceptual content, which is given to us from with-out, thought content appears from within. We shall call the form in which thought content arises "intuition." Intuition is to thinking as observation is to perceiving. Intuition and observation are our two sources of knowledge. We remain alienated from an object in the observed world as long as we do not have within us the correspond-ing intuition, which supplies the piece of reality missing from the percept. Full reality remains closed off to anyone without the ability to find intuitions corresponding to things. Just as a color-blind per-son sees only shades of brilliance without hues, a person without intuition observes only unconnected perceptual fragments.

THINKING AND FEELING

Thinking and feeling correspond to the dual nature of our being.... Thinking is the element through which we participate in the universal process of the cosmos; feeling is the element through which we can withdraw into the confines of our own being.

Our thinking unites us with the world; our feeling leads us back into ourselves and makes us individuals. If we were only thinking and perceiving beings, then our whole life would flow past in monotonous indifference. If we could only know ourselves as selves, then we would be completely indifferent to ourselves. It is only because we have self-feeling along with self-cognition, and pleasure and pain along with the perception of things, that we live as individual beings whose existence is not limited to our conceptual relationship to the rest of the world, but who also have special value for ourselves. Some might be tempted to see in the life of feeling an element more richly imbued with reality than thinking contemplation of the world. The reply to this is that the life of feeling has this richer meaning only for my individuality. For the world as a whole, my feeling life can attain value only if the feeling, as a percept of my self, combines with a concept and so integrates itself indirectly into the cosmos.

REAL KNOWLEDGE

Any increase or alteration in the human senses would result in a different perceptual picture—an enrichment or alteration of human experience. But real knowledge must be achieved, even in regard to this experience, by the interaction of percept and concept. The deepening of cognition depends on the forces of intuition that live in thinking. In the experience of thinking, such intuition can immerse itself either more or less deeply in reality.

EVERYTHING GIVEN IS A PERCEPT

The idea of the percept ... must not be confused with that of external sense perception, which is only a special case of it.... Everything, both sensory and spiritual, that meets a human being is here taken to be a "percept" until it is grasped by the actively elaborated concept.

THINKING, FEELING, WILLING

The difficulty of grasping thinking in its essence by observing it consists in this: When the soul wants to bring it into the focus of attention, this essence has all too easily already slipped away from the observing soul. All that is left for the soul is the dead abstraction, the corpse of living thinking. If we look only at this abstraction, we can easily feel drawn to the mysticism of feeling or the metaphysics of will, which seem so "full of life." We find it strange if anyone seeks to grasp the essence of reality in "mere thoughts." But whoever truly manages experience life in thinking sees that dwelling in mere feeling or contemplating the element of will cannot even be compared (let alone ranked above) the inner richness and the experience, the inner calmness and mobility, in the life of thinking.

It is precisely the richness, the inner fullness of the experience of thinking that makes its reflection in normal consciousness seem dead and abstract. No other activity of the human soul is so easily misunderstood as thinking....

Thinking all too easily leaves us cold. It seems to dry out the life of the soul. But this is only the sharply contoured shadow of the reality of thinking—a reality interwoven with light, dipping down warmly into the phenomena of the world. This dipping down occurs with a power that flows forth in the activity of thinking itself—the power of love in spiritual form.

One should not object that to speak of love in active thinking is to displace a feeling—love—into thinking.... Whoever turns toward essential thinking finds within it both will and feeling, and both of these in the depths of their reality. Whoever turns aside from thinking toward "pure" feeling and willing loses the true reality of feeling and willing. If we experience thinking intuitively, we also do justice to the experience of feeling and willing.

A Self-Supporting Spiritual Entity

To observe thinking is to live, during the observation, immediately within the weaving of a self-supporting spiritual entity. We could even say that those who want to grasp the essence of the spirit as it first presents itself to human beings can do so in the self-sustaining activity of thinking.

✻

If we see what is really present in thinking, we will recognize that only one part of reality is present in the percept and that we experience the other part—which belongs to it and is necessary for it to appear as full reality—in the permeation of the percept by thinking. We shall see, then, in what appears in consciousness, not a shadowy copy of reality, but a spiritual essence that sustains itself. Of this spiritual essence we can say that it becomes present to our consciousness through intuition. Intuition is the conscious experience, within what is purely spiritual, of a purely spiritual content. The essence of thinking can be grasped only through intuition.

THINKING'S DOUBLE FUNCTION

The effective essence of thinking has a double function. First, it represses the human organization's own activity. Second, it replaces that activity with itself.

"I" AND I-CONSCIOUSNESS

What happens in the human organization as a result of thinking has nothing to do with the essence of thinking, but it does have something to do with the origin of I-consciousness out of thinking. The real "I" certainly lies within the essence of one's thinking, but I-consciousness does not. Anyone who observes thinking without prejudice sees this is the case. The "I" is to be found in thinking; but I-consciousness appears because the traces of thinking activity are engraved in general consciousness.... I-consciousness therefore arises through the bodily organization.... Once it arises, it is taken up into thinking, and thereafter shares in the spiritual being of thinking.

THINKING WITHOUT CONTENT (OR OBJECT)

The highest stage of individual life is conceptual thinking without reference to a specific perceptual content. We determine the content of a concept out of the conceptual sphere through pure intuition.

ETHICAL INDIVIDUALISM

The sum of ideas active within us, the real content of our intuitions, constitutes what is individual in us, not withstanding the universality of the world of ideas. To the extent that the intuitive content turns into action, it is the ethical content of the individual. Allowing this intuitive content to live itself out fully is the driving force of morality.

*

Only an act of will arising from an intuition can be individual.

WHAT IS INDIVIDUAL IN ME?

What is individual in me is not my organism, with its drives and feelings, but my world of ideas that lights up within this organism.

FREEDOM

Insofar as an action proceeds from the conceptual part of my individual being, it is felt to be free. Every other portion of an action ... is felt to be unfree.

CODA

Eternal becoming in thinking,
Each step, at the same time a deepening
Overcoming the surface,
Penetrating the depths.

—Inscription in *The Philosophy of Freedom*, 1894

The Way of Reverence
and Its Fruits

Reverence, as Rudolf Steiner never tired of repeating, is the fundamental condition for all spiritual development. "Mentioned in all religions," confirmed by "every practical and experienced esotericist and occultist," it is perhaps best expressed by the Gospel injunction: "Except ye become ... as little children, ye shall not enter the kingdom of heaven" (Matt. 18:3). Accordingly, "Every esotericist must penetrate this well-known saying to the very essence." Reverence, according to Steiner, "is the force—the magnetic power—that raises us to higher spheres of suprasensory life. It is a law of the spiritual world that all who seek the higher life must inscribe with golden letters into their souls. Inner development must start from this basic mood of the soul. Without this feeling of reverence, nothing can be achieved" (November 7, 1905). The following sentences are from *How to Know Higher Worlds*.

REVERENCE: THE FUNDAMENTAL MOOD

We begin with a fundamental mood of the soul. Spiritual researchers call this basic attitude *the path of reverence*, of devotion to truth and to knowledge. Only those who have acquired this fundamental mood or attitude can become pupils in an esoteric school.

A HOLY PLACE

Have you ever stood before the door of someone you revered, filled with holy awe as you turned the doorknob to enter for the first time a room that was a "holy place" for you? Then the feeling you experienced at that moment is the seed that can later blossom.

HUMILITY

Only a person who has passed through the gate of humility can ascend to the heights of the spirit.

DEVOTION AND RESPECT

To be students of this path, we must train ourselves in the mood of devotion. We must seek—in all things around us, in all our experiences—for what can arouse our admiration and respect. If I meet other people and criticize their weaknesses, I rob myself of higher cognitive power. But if I try to enter deeply and lovingly into another person's good qualities, I gather in that force.

We must always bear in mind the need to cultivate such admiration and respect. Experienced seekers know what strength they gain by always looking for the good in everything and withholding critical judgment. This practice should not remain simply an outer rule of life, but must take hold of the innermost part of the soul. It lies in us to perfect ourselves and gradually transform ourselves completely. But this transformation must take place in our innermost depths, in our *thinking*. Showing respect outwardly in our relations with other beings is not enough; we must carry this respect into our thoughts. Therefore we must begin our inner schooling by bringing devotion into our thought life. We must guard against disrespectful, disparaging, and criticizing thoughts. We must try to practice reverence and devotion in our thinking at all times.

SEEING DIFFERENTLY: OPENING OUR SPIRITUAL EYES

Each moment that we spend becoming aware of the derogatory, judgmental, and critical opinions that still remain in our consciousness brings us closer to higher knowledge. We will advance even more quickly if, in such moments, we fill our consciousness with admiration, respect, and reverence for the world and life. Those experienced in such matters know that these moments awaken forces in us that otherwise remain dormant. Filling our consciousness in this way opens our spiritual eyes. We begin to see things around us that we could not see before. We begin to realize that previously we saw only a part of the world surrounding us. We begin to see our fellow human beings in a different way than we did before.

DEVELOPING AN INNER LIFE

What we attain through devotion becomes even more effective when another kind of feeling is added. This consists in learning to surrender ourselves less and less to the impressions of the outer world and instead developing an active inner life. If we chase after amusements and rush from one sensory impression to the next, we will not find the way to esoteric knowledge. It is not that students should become dull or unfeeling toward the outer world; rather, *a rich inner life* should orient us in responding to impressions.

A person rich in feeling and deep of soul who passes through a beautiful mountain landscape will have a different experience from one whose inner life is poor in feeling. *Inner experience is the only key to the outer world's beauties.* When we travel overseas, whether only a few inner experiences pass through our souls or whether we sense the eternal language of the world spirit and understand the mysterious riddles of creation depends upon how our inner lives have been developed. To develop a meaningful relationship to the outer world, we must learn to work with our own feelings and ideas. The world around us is filled everywhere with the glory of God, but we have to experience the divine in our own souls before we can find it in our surroundings. As students on the path, we are told to create moments in life when we can withdraw into ourselves in silence and solitude. In these moments, we should not surrender to our own concerns; to do so leads us away from what we are striving for. In such moments, we should instead allow what we have experienced—what the outer world has told us—to linger on in complete stillness. In such quiet moments, every flower, every animal, and every action will disclose undreamed mysteries. This prepares us to receive new sensory impressions of the outer world with completely different eyes.

A FUNDAMENTAL PRINCIPLE

One fundamental principle, taught in every form of training, must never be violated if we wish to achieve our goal. This principle states: *Every insight that you seek in order to enrich only your own store of learning and to accumulate treasure for yourself alone leads you from your path. But every insight you seek in order to become more mature on the path for the ennoblement of human and world evolution takes you one step forward.* This fundamental law must always be observed. Only if we make it the guiding principle of our lives can we call ourselves true seekers after higher knowledge. This truth of esoteric training may be summarized as follows: *Every idea that does not become an ideal for you kills a force in your soul, but every idea that becomes an ideal for you creates forces of life within you.*

INNER PEACE

One of the first rules may now be put into words somewhat as follows: Create moments of inner peace for yourself, and in these moments learn to *distinguish the essential from the inessential.*

DEVELOPING A HIGHER POINT OF VIEW

As students of the spirit, we must set aside a brief period of time in daily life during which to focus on matters that are quite different from the objects of our daily activity. The kind of activity we engage in must also differ from what occupies the rest of our day.

This is not to say, however, that what we do in the minutes we have set aside is unconnected with the substance of our daily work. On the contrary, we soon realize that, if approached correctly, such moments give us the full strength for completing our daily tasks. We need not fear that following this rule will take time away from our duties. If someone really cannot spare any more time, five minutes a day are enough. The important thing is how we use those five minutes.

In these moments, we should tear ourselves completely away from our everyday life. Our thinking and feeling lives should have a quite different coloring than usual. We should allow our joys, sorrows, worries, experiences, and actions to pass before our soul, but our attitude should be one of looking at everything we have experienced from a higher point of view. Consider how, in ordinary life, our perception of what other people have experienced or done is different from the way we perceive our own experiences or actions. This must be so. We are still interwoven with what we experience or do, but we are only observers of other's experiences or actions. During the time we set aside for ourselves, then, we must try to view and judge our own experiences and actions as if they belonged to someone else.

VIEWING OURSELVES AS STRANGERS

As students of higher knowledge, we must find the strength to view ourselves as we would strangers; we must face ourselves with the inner tranquillity of a judge. If we achieve this, our experiences will reveal themselves in a new light. As long as we are still woven into our experiences and stand within them, we will remain just as attached to the nonessential as we are to the essential. But once we attain the inner peace of the overview, the nonessential separates itself from the essential. Sorrow and joy, every thought, and every decision will look different when we face ourselves in this way.

✧

As we progress in this direction, we are increasingly able to control the way impressions from the outer world affect us. For example, we may hear someone say something to hurt or anger us. Before we began esoteric training, this would have made us feel hurt or anger. Now, however, because we are on the path of inner development, we can take the hurtful or annoying sting out of such words before they reach our inner being. Another example: before beginning to follow this path, we may have been quick to lose patience while waiting for something. But now, having started on the path and become students in a school of esoteric study, in our contemplative moments we imbue ourselves fully with the realization that impatience is generally futile, so that, whenever we feel any impatience, it immediately recalls this realization to mind. The impatience that was about to take root thus disappears, and the time we might have wasted in expressions of impatience can now be filled with the useful observation we may make while waiting.

A BLISS-BESTOWING WORLD

Something else is also needed. When we view ourselves as strangers, it is still only *ourselves* that we contemplate. We see the experiences and actions connected to us by the particular course of life we have grown through. But we must go beyond that. We must rise to see the purely human level that no longer has anything to do with our own particular situation. We must reach the point of contemplating those things that concern us as human beings as such, completely independent of the circumstances and conditions of our particular life.

As we do this, something comes to life in us that transcends what is personal or individual. Our view is directed toward worlds higher than those our everyday life brings us. We begin to feel and experience that we belong to these higher worlds, of which our senses and everyday activities can tell us nothing. The center of our being shifts inward. We listen to the voices that speak within us during moments of serenity. Inwardly, we associate with the spiritual world. Removed from our daily round of life, we become deaf to its noise; everything around us becomes still. We put aside everything that reminds us of outer impressions. Quiet, inner contemplation and dialog with the purely spiritual world completely fill our soul.

For students of the spirit, this quiet contemplation must become a necessity of life. Initially, we are wholly absorbed in a world of thought. We must develop a *living feeling* for this silent thinking activity. *We must learn to love what flows toward us from the spirit.* Then we quickly cease to accept this thought world as less real than the ordinary life around us. Instead, we begin to work with our thoughts as we do with material objects. Then the moment will come when we begin to realize that what is revealed to us in the silence of inner thinking activity is more real than the physical objects around us. We experience that *life* speaks in this world of thoughts.

We realize that thoughts are not mere shadow pictures and that hidden *beings* speak to us through thoughts. Out of the silence something begins to speak to us. Previously, we could hear speech only with our ears, but now words sound within our souls. An inner speech, or inner word, is disclosed to us. The first time we experience this, we feel supremely blessed. Our outer world is suffused with an inner light. A second life begins for us. A divine, bliss-bestowing world streams through us.

CLARITY AND PRECISION IN MEDITATION

We should not lose ourselves in feelings during these moments of meditation. Nor should our souls be filled with vague sensations. This would only keep us from attaining true spiritual insight. Our thoughts should be clear, sharp, and precise. We will find a way of achieving this when we no longer remain blindly with the thoughts that arise in us. We should fill ourselves instead with high thoughts that more advanced and spiritually inspired souls have thought in similar moments. Here our starting point should be writings that have grown out of meditative revelations. We may find such texts in the literature of mystics, Gnostics, or spiritual science. Such texts provide the material for our meditations. After all, it is seekers of the spirit who have set down the thoughts of divine science in such works. Indeed, it is through these messengers that the spirit has permitted these thoughts to be made known to the world.

LEARNING TO SEE INTO THE SPIRITUAL WORLD

The first step is to direct the soul's attention toward certain processes in the world around us. These processes are *life, as it buds, grows, and flourishes*; and, on the other hand, all phenomena connected with *withering, fading, and dying away*. Wherever we turn our eyes, these two processes are present together. By their nature, they always evoke feelings and thoughts in us. Normally, however, we do not give ourselves sufficiently to these feelings and thoughts. We rush from one sensory impression to the next. Now, however, we must consciously and intensively focus fully on them. Whenever we perceive a quite definite form of blossoming and flourishing, we must banish all else from our souls and, for a short time, dwell on this one impression alone. As we do so, we soon realize that a feeling, which previously merely flitted through our souls, has now grown and become strong and full of energy. We must let this feeling quietly echo within us. We must become completely still inwardly. Cutting ourselves off from the rest of the world around us, we must attend only to what the soul can tell us about the facts of blossoming and flourishing.

CULTIVATING CERTAIN FEELINGS

First, we must look at phenomena as actively and precisely as possible. Only then should we devote ourselves to the feelings coming to life in our souls and to the thoughts arising there. It is essential that we give our attention to both feelings and thoughts as they arise in complete inner equilibrium.

If we find the necessary inner peace, surrendering ourselves to what comes to life in our souls, then after a certain time we will experience the following. We will notice, rising within us, new kinds of feelings and thoughts that we never knew before. The more often we focus our attention—first on something growing and flourishing, and then on something withering and dying—the more lively and active these feelings will become. Eventually, organs of clairvoyant "seeing" are formed out of the feelings and thoughts that arise in relation to growing and flourishing and withering and dying, just as the eyes and ears of our physical organism are formed by natural forces out of inanimate matter.

If we cultivate our feeling life in this way, we will find that a specific form of feeling is connected to the processes of growing and becoming, whereas a very different one is attached to those of withering and dying. These forms of feeling may be described, though only approximately. Each student may obtain a complete idea of these feelings, however, by going through the inner experience. Those who repeatedly direct their attention to the processes of becoming, flourishing, and blossoming will feel something faintly resembling the sensation we experience as we watch the sun rise. The processes of withering and dying, on the other hand, produce an experience that may be compared with what we feel as we watch the moon slowly rise on the horizon.

Cultivated appropriately and trained in an ever livelier and more active way, these two types of feeling become forces that can lead to the most significant spiritual effects. Deliberately, regularly, and repeatedly surrendering to such feelings, we find a new world opening before us. The soul world or so-called astral plane begins to dawn. Growth and decay are now no longer merely facts that evoke vague impressions; rather, they form definite spiritual lines and figures we had no inkling of before. Moreover, these lines and figures change their forms with the phenomena. A blossoming flower conjures up a particular line before our souls, while a grow-ing animal or a dying tree gives rise to other lines. In this way, the soul world (or astral plane) spreads out before us.

ORIENTATION

Another important point is what esoteric science calls "orienta-tion" in the higher worlds. We achieve such an orientation once we have completely filled ourselves with the consciousness that feel-ings and thoughts are real facts, just as real as tables and chairs are in the physical sensory world. In the worlds of soul and thought, feelings and thoughts affect each other, just as sensory phenomena do in the physical world. Unless we are actively filled with the con-sciousness that thoughts and feelings are real, we cannot believe that entertaining a wrong thought can be devastating to the other thoughts that occupy our world of thinking, just as a bullet shot blindly from a rifle destroys the things it hits in the physical world. Thus, although we might never allow ourselves to engage in visible actions that we consider meaningless, we nonetheless do not shrink from entertaining wrong thoughts or feelings, because we do not see them as dangerous to the rest of the world.

To move forward on the path to higher knowledge and advance in spiritual science, we must therefore pay as careful attention to our thoughts and feelings as we do to our movements in the physical world. For instance, we do not usually try to go straight through a wall, but direct our steps around it; in other words, we obey the laws of the physical world. Likewise, the world of feelings and thoughts has its own laws, but they do not force themselves upon us from the outside; instead, they must flow from the life of the soul.

For this to occur, we must never allow ourselves false thoughts and feelings. Random musings, playful daydreams, and the arbi-trary ebb and flow of feeling must all be banished from the soul. We need not fear that this will make us unfeeling; on the contrary, we find that we become truly rich in feelings and creative in real imagination only when we regulate our inner life in this way. Important feelings and fruitful thoughts then replace the petty indulgence of emotions and the play of associating ideas. These, in turn, help us gain an orientation in the spiritual world, allowing us to enter the right relationship with its phenomena. And this, too, has a definite, noticeable effect.

SOUNDS

Students must also direct their attention to the world of *sounds*. Here we distinguish between sounds produced by so-called inanimate objects (a falling object, a bell, or a musical instrument) and sounds that come from living beings, whether animals or people. When we hear a bell, we perceive the sound and associate it with a pleasant feeling. The scream of an animal, on the other hand, not only evokes an emotional association but also reveals the animal's inner experience—its pleasure or pain. In esoteric training, we focus on the second type of sound, concentrating our whole attention on the fact that the sound communicates something outside our own souls.

LISTENING

We must immerse ourselves in this "otherness" and inwardly unite our feelings with the pain or pleasure expressed by the sound. To do this, we must disregard what the sound is *for us*—whether pleasant or unpleasant, agreeable or disagreeable. Our soul must be filled only with what is happening in the being making the sound. As we practice this exercise systematically and deliberately, we acquire the faculty of merging, as it were, with the being that made the sound. Naturally, a musically sensitive person will find this particular exercise for cultivating the soul life easier than one who is not musically inclined. But no one should think that a musical ear is a substitute for doing the exercise systematically. As occult students, our goal is to come to feel toward the whole of nature in this way.

Something else must be added to this practice before we can attain the highest point in this area of soul experience. As we develop as esoteric students, it is especially important that we also work on the way we listen to other people when they speak. On the path to higher knowledge, listening skill is extremely important. We must become accustomed to listening so that we quiet our own inner life completely when we listen. In general, when someone states an opinion and another listens, agreement or disagreement stirs immediately within the listener. We often feel compelled to express our own opinion at once, especially if we disagree. However, on the path to higher knowledge we must learn to silence any agreement or disagreement with the opinions we hear. Naturally, this does not mean that we should suddenly change our way of life and strive to achieve this complete inner silence all the time. We must start with isolated instances that we choose intentionally. Then, slowly and gradually, as if by itself, this new way of listening becomes a habit.

In spiritual research, we practice this new way of listening in a systematic way. As students, we should feel it our duty to set aside, as an exercise, certain times when we listen to the most contrary opinions, completely silencing within us all agreement and, especially, all negative judgments. Not only must we silence our intellectual judgment but also any feelings of disapproval, rejection, or even agreement. Above all, we must observe ourselves carefully to ensure that such feelings, even though absent from the surface of the soul, are not present in its innermost depths. For example, we must learn to listen to the remarks of those who are in some way inferior to us, suppressing *every* feeling of superiority or knowing better.

Listening to children in this way is especially useful, and even the wisest of us can learn a great deal from them. These exercises teach us to listen selflessly to the words of others, completely excluding our own personality, opinions, and feelings. Once we are practiced in listening in this way without criticism, then, even when the most contradictory views and illogical statements are aired before us, we gradually begin to learn to unite ourselves with the being of another, entering it fully. We begin to hear *through* the words, into the other's soul. If we practice this new habit consistently, sound becomes the medium through which we can perceive soul and spirit.

SPIRITUAL STUDY

All higher truths are attained only through such inward prompting. Whatever we hear from the lips of true spiritual researchers is only what they have brought to experience in this way. This does not mean that it is unnecessary to study esoteric literature before we are able to hear this "inner word." On the contrary, reading such writings and listening to the teachings of esoteric researchers are themselves a means of achieving knowledge. Indeed, every statement of spiritual science that we hear is meant to guide the mind in the direction necessary for the soul to experience true progress. Therefore the exercises described here should be accompanied by the intensive study of what researchers in spiritual science bring to the world. Such study is part of the preparatory work in all schools of esoteric training.

ILLUMINATION

The stage of illumination starts from very simple processes. Here, too, as in the stage of preparation, it is a matter of developing and awakening certain feelings and thoughts latent in every one of us. Anyone who focuses on these simple processes with persistence, rigor, and complete patience will be led to a perception of the inner manifestations of light.

We begin by examining various natural objects in a particular way—for example, a transparent, beautifully shaped stone (a crystal), a plant, and an animal. First, we try to direct our whole attention to comparing a stone with an animal. The thoughts we form in making this comparison must pass through the soul, accompanied by lively *feelings.* No other thoughts or feelings must be allowed to intrude and disturb our intense, attentive observation. We should say to ourselves: "The stone has a form; the animal also has a form. The stone stays peacefully in place; the animal changes places. It is instinct (or desire) that moves the animal to move. Instincts are also served by the animal's form. Its organs and limbs are shaped by these instincts. Stones, on the other hand, are not shaped by desires but by a force without desire."

As we closely observe the stone and animal and immerse ourselves intensely in such thoughts, two very different kinds of feeling come to life in the soul. One kind streams into the soul from the stone, another from the animal. Although this exercise will probably not succeed in the beginning, if we practice with real patience, these two feelings will gradually appear. We need only practice the exercise again and again. At first, the feelings persist only as long as the observation lasts. Later, they continue to work on after the exercise is over. Eventually, they become something that remains alive in our souls. At that point, we need only reflect again, and the stone and animal feelings will arise again, even without contemplating the external object. Organs of clairvoyance are formed from these feelings and the accompanying thoughts.

If we add plants to our observations, we notice that the feeling flowing from the plant, both in nature and intensity, is midway between the feelings that flow from a stone and an animal. The organs built up in this way are *spiritual eyes.* They gradually allow us to see soul and spiritual colors. But the lines and figures of the spiritual world remain dark as long as we have not claimed what was previously described as the path or stage of "preparation." Through the process of illumination, they become light. Again, it must be noted that words such as *dark* and *light,* as well as other expressions, are only approximations of the intended meaning.

Ordinary languages were created for physical relationships. If we use ordinary language, as we must, only approximations of spiritual phenomena are possible.

A Seed Meditation

We place before us a small seed from a plant. Starting with this insignificant object, the point is to think the right thoughts intensively, and by means of these thoughts to develop certain feelings.

First, we establish what we are really seeing with our eyes. We describe to ourselves the form, color, and other properties of the seed. Then we ponder the thought: "This seed, if planted in the ground, will grow into a complex plant." We visualize the plant; we make it present to and within us. We build it up in imagination. Then we think: "What I am now visualizing in my imagination, the forces of earth and light will later draw forth, in reality, from this small seed. But if this were an artificial seed, an artificial copy so perfect that my eyes could not distinguish it from a real seed, then no forces of earth and light would ever be able to draw forth such a plant from it." If we can clearly form this thought and bring it to life within us, then we will be able to form the next thought easily, and with the right feeling: "Already concealed within this seed—as the force of the whole plant—is what will later grow out of it. An artificial copy of the seed has no such force. Yet, to my eyes, both seeds look the same. Therefore the real seed contains something invisible that is absent in the copy."

Thoughts and feelings should now focus on this invisible reality. We must imagine that this invisible force or reality will, in time, change into a visible plant whose color and form we will be able to see. We should hold this thought: "The invisible will become visible. If I were unable to think, then what later becomes visible could not announce itself to me now."

It is important to emphasize that whatever we think we must also feel with intensity. Meditative thoughts need to be experienced calmly and peacefully. No other thoughts should distract us. Time should be allowed for both the thought and the feeling united with it to penetrate the soul. If this is done in the right way, then after a time—perhaps only after many unsuccessful attempts—we become conscious of a new force within us. This creates a new perception. The seed seems to be enclosed in a small cloud of light. In a sensory-spiritual way, we sense it as a kind of flame. At its center, we experience a sensation similar to the impression made by the color purple, at its edges a sensation similar to the color blue.

What we could not see before now becomes apparent to us, created by the force of the thoughts and feelings that we have awakened within us. The plant—which is still physically invisible and will not become visible until later—is revealed to us in a spiritually visible manner.

A PLANT MEDITATION

Another exercise connected to the seed meditation is the following. We place before us a mature plant. First, we immerse ourselves in the thought: "A time will come when this plant will wither and decay. Everything I see now will no longer exist then. But the plant will have produced seeds, and these will become new plants. Thus I again become aware of something I cannot see that is hidden in what I can see." We imbue ourselves with the thought: "Soon, the plant form with all its colors will no longer be there. But knowing that the plant produces seeds teaches me that it will not disappear into nothingness. I cannot see what preserves the plant from disappearing, anymore than I could see the future plant in the seed. It follows, therefore, that something else is in the plant that I cannot see with my eyes. If I let this thought live in me, and if the appropriate feeling unites with it, then after awhile, new force will grow in my soul and become a new perception." A kind of spiritual flame form will grow out of the plant. Of course, this flame will be correspondingly larger than the one described in the case of the seed. It will be felt as blue-green at its center and as yellowish-red at the periphery.

A Fundamental Law

Once we have discovered in ourselves the fundamentals of spiritual perception, we can go on to contemplate our fellow human beings. We begin by selecting a simple phenomena connected with human life. But first, we must work seriously and with sincerity on the integrity of our moral character. We must remove all thoughts of ever using the knowledge we gain in this way for our own self-interest. We must firmly decide never to make evil use of any power we might gain over other people. Thus, if we seek to penetrate the mysteries of human nature through our own efforts, we must abide by the golden rule of the occult sciences. *"For every single step that you take in seeking knowledge of hidden truths, you must take three steps in perfecting your character toward goodness."* Those who follow this rule can do the following exercises:

> We visualize a person we have seen wishing for something, and we direct our attention to this desire. It is best to recall the moment when the desire was strongest, and we did not know yet whether the person would satisfy the desire. Then we surrender to this picture, completely dedicated to what we can observe in our memory. In our soul, we create the greatest imaginable inner calm. We try, as far as possible, to ignore everything else going on around us. Above all, we pay close attention to any feeling awakened in our soul by the mental image we have formed. Then we allow this feeling to arise within us, like a cloud on an otherwise empty horizon.

Keeping Silent

Know how to be silent about your spiritual perceptions. Even be silent about them with yourself. Do not try to clothe in words what you see in the spirit. Do not try to understand it with your ordinary, unskilled reason; give yourself fully to your spiritual perception, and do not disturb it with too much pondering. Remember that your thinking has not yet reached the level of your spiritual vision. You have acquired this thinking in a life that until now has been limited wholly to the physical world. But what you are now acquiring goes beyond that. Therefore do not try to measure these new, higher perceptions according to the standard used to measure your old ones.

CODA: GENERAL REQUIREMENTS FOR A SPIRITUAL PATH

What follows is a description of the series of conditions to be met by the student. It should be noted that none of these requires complete perfection; we need only strive toward that goal. No one can fulfill these conditions completely, but everyone can set out on the path to their fulfillment. It is our attitude and our will to begin that are important....

FIRST REQUIREMENT: *Dedication to Self-Improvement*

The first requirement is that we turn our attention to the improvement of our physical and mental or spiritual health.

SECOND REQUIREMENT: *To be a Part of the Whole of Life*

The second requirement is to feel ourselves a part of the whole of life.

THIRD REQUIREMENT: *The Reality of Thoughts and Feelings*

The third requirement requires that we win through to the conviction that thoughts and feelings are as important for the world as actions. We should recognize that, when we hate our fellow human beings, it is just as destructive as physically striking them. This brings us again to the insight that anything we do for our own improvement benefits not just ourselves but also the world.

The world benefits just as much from pure feelings and thoughts as from good actions. Indeed, as long as we do not recognize the significance that one's inner life has for the world, we are unprepared to take up esoteric training. And we cannot rightly believe in the meaning of our inner lives, our souls, until we care for our souls and perform our inner work as if it were at least as real as our outer work. We must know that what we feel has as much impact upon the world as the work done by our hands.

THE FOURTH REQUIREMENT: *The Spiritual Scales*

We must acquire the conviction that our true nature is not outside but within. We can achieve nothing spiritually if we regard ourselves merely as a product, a result, of the physical world. The very basis of esoteric training is feeling that we are soul-spiritual beings. Once we have made this feeling our own, we are ready to distinguish between our inner sense of duty and outer success. We learn to recognize that there is no necessary and immediate correlation between these. As esoteric students, we must find the middle ground between following the demands of the world and doing what we see as the right thing to do. We must not force upon others something that they cannot understand. At the same time, however, we must be free of the urge to do only what those around us recognize and approve of. Only the inner voice of the soul, as it honestly strives for higher knowledge, can confirm our truths. Yet we must also learn as much as possible about our environment and find out what is useful and good for it. And, if we do so, we will develop within ourselves what esoteric science calls "the spiritual scales" or the "balance"—on one of whose trays lies a helpful heart, open to the needs of the world, and on the other, inner firmness and unshakable endurance.

THE FIFTH REQUIREMENT: *Steadfastness*

This brings us to the fifth requirement: steadfastness in following through on a resolution once it has been made. Nothing should lead us to abandon something we have decided upon except the insight that we made a mistake. Each resolution is a force that works in its own way—even when it is not immediately successful in the area where it is first applied. Success is crucial only when we act out of longing. But any action motivated by craving is worthless from the point of view of the higher world. In the higher world, love is the only motivation for action. As esoteric students, all that stirs us to action must be subsumed in love. If we act out of love, we will never tire of transforming our resolutions into actions, no matter how often we may have failed in the past.

As a result, we do not judge an action based on its *outer* effect on others, but take satisfaction in the activity of performing our actions. We must learn to offer up our actions, our very essence, to the world—regardless of how our offering is received. Esoteric students must be prepared for this life of sacrifice and service.

The Sixth Requirement: *Gratitude*

The sixth requirement is that we develop the feeling of gratitude for all that we receive. We should know that our very existence is a gift from the whole universe. How much is necessary for human beings to receive and sustain their existence! We owe so much to nature and to others. Grateful thoughts such as these must become second nature for those engaged in esoteric training. If we do not give ourselves fully to such thoughts, we will never develop the *all-embracing love* needed to attain higher knowledge. Unless I love something, it cannot reveal itself to me. And every revelation should fill me with thankfulness, for I am made richer by it.

The Seventh Requirement: *Harmony*

The first six requirements come together in the seventh: always to understand life as these conditions demand. In so doing, we create the possibility of giving our lives the stamp of unity. All the different expressions of our life will then be in harmony and not contradict each other. And this will prepare us for the calm, inner peace we must develop during the first steps in esoteric training.

Developing the Chakras, or "Lotus Flowers"

One way of talking about inner development uses the spiritual physiology of the chakras. At the center of *How to Know Higher Worlds*, Steiner gives a series of exercises, specifically presented in terms of "developing the chakras," though all exercises in fact "develop" them. The chakras (literally, "wheels") are suprasensory organs, interfused with the various suprasensory bodies (etheric, astral, "I"). They are points of concentration, or rotating vortices, in wheel or flower form, distinguishable by location and number of petals. There are traditionally seven main chakras, twenty-one secondary chakras, and a great number of smaller chakras (corresponding more or less to acupuncture meridians). The seven main chakras are: the four-petalled or root chakra at the base of the coccyx, the six-petalled or sacral (sex) chakra, the ten-petalled or solar plexus chakra, the twelve-petalled or heart chakra, the sixteen-petalled or throat chakra, the two-petalled or forehead chakra, and the thousand-petalled or crown chakra. Steiner's chakra teaching differs from traditional teaching in several ways. For instance, he goes from top to bottom, rather than the other way; and he speaks of an eight-petalled chakra. (For much more on this, see Florin Lowndes, *Enlivening the Chakra of the Heart*.).

Our suprasensory form

The further we advance in soul development, the more regularly structured our soul organism becomes. This organism remains confused and unstructured in a person whose soul life is still undeveloped.

Yet even in such an unstructured soul organism a clairvoyant can still see a form that stands out clearly from its surroundings. The form extends from the inside of the head to the middle of the physical body. To the clairvoyant it looks like an independent body, containing certain organs. These organs—which we shall now consider—may be seen spiritually in the following areas of the physical body: the first, between the eyes; the second, near the larynx; the third, in the region of the heart; the fourth, in the neighborhood of the pit of the stomach or solar plexus; and the fifth and the sixth, in the lower abdomen or reproductive region.

Because they resemble wheels or flowers, esotericists call these formations *chakras* (wheels) or "lotus flowers." But these expressions are no more accurate than calling the parts of a building "wings." In both cases, we are dealing only with figures of speech, with analogies. In a person whose soul life is undeveloped, the "lotus flowers" are of a darkish color, quiet and unmoving. In a seer, they are in motion, shining forth in different colors. With some differences, the same occurs in the case of mediums—but this does not concern us here.

One of the occurrences when an esoteric student begins practicing the exercises is that the light of the lotus flowers intensifies; later the flowers will also begin to rotate. When this happens, it means that a person is beginning to have the ability to see clairvoyantly. These "flowers" are the sense organs of the soul. Their rotation indicates that we are able to perceive the suprasensory realm. Until we have developed the astral senses in this way, we cannot see anything suprasensory.

The spiritual sense organ, which is situated near the larynx, enables us to see clairvoyantly into the way of thinking of other soul beings. It also allows us a deeper insight into the true laws of natural phenomena, while the organ located in the region of the heart opens clairvoyant cognition into the mentality and character of other souls. Whoever has developed this organ is also able to cognize certain deeper forces in plants and animals. With the sense organ situated near the solar plexus, we gain insight into the abilities and talents of other souls and see what role animals, plants, minerals, metals, atmospheric phenomena, and so on play in the household of nature.

The organ in the vicinity of the larynx has sixteen "petals" or "spokes"; the one near the heart, twelve; and the one near the solar plexus, ten.

Specific soul activities are connected with the development of these sense organs. Whoever practices these activities in a particular way contributes to the development of the corresponding spiritual sense organ. For example, eight of the sixteen petals of the "sixteen-petalled lotus flower" near the larynx were formed in the distant past, in an earlier evolutionary stage. We ourselves contributed nothing to their development. We received these first eight petals as a gift of nature at a time when human consciousness was still dreamlike and dull. These eight petals were already active then, and their activities corresponded to this state of dim consciousness. As consciousness intensified, these lotus petals then lost their light and ceased their activity. We ourselves can form the remaining eight petals through the conscious practice of exercises. This will make the whole lotus flower shining and mobile.

The acquisition of specific faculties depends upon the development of each of these sixteen lotus petals. As already implied, however, we can develop only eight of these petals consciously. The other eight then appear of their own accord.

Eight soul processes to develop the sixteen-petalled lotus flower

To develop the *sixteen-petalled lotus flower*, we direct our care and attention to *eight specific soul processes* that we usually perform without care or attention.

The first soul process concerns the way we acquire ideas or mental images. As a rule, this is left to chance. We happen to see or hear something, and on that basis we form concepts. As long as we behave in this way, the sixteen-petalled lotus flower remains inactive. But once we begin to discipline ourselves, it begins to move. Discipline here means paying attention to our ideas or mental representations; each must become meaningful to us. We must begin to see in every image or idea a specific message about something in the outer world. Ideas that do not have a meaning for the outer world should no longer satisfy us. We must guide our conceptual life to become a true mirror of the outer world. All striving must eliminate false ideas from the soul.

The second soul process to be considered—in much the same way as the first—is how we make decisions. Any decision, even the most trivial, should be made only after thorough, well-reasoned deliberation. We should remove all thoughtless activity and meaningless action from our souls. We must have well-reasoned purpose for all that we do. Anything that we cannot find a reason for must not be done.

The third soul process concerns speech. When we are esoteric students, every word should have substance and meaning. Talk for the sake of talking diverts us from the path. We must avoid the ordinary kind of conversation, in which everyone talks at the same time and topics are randomly jumbled together. This does not mean that we should cut ourselves off from interaction with others. On the contrary, it is precisely in interaction with others that we should learn to make our words meaningful. We should be ready to speak to and answer everyone, but only after having taken thought and thoroughly considered the issue at hand. We should never speak without good reason. We should talk neither too much nor too little.

The fourth soul process concerns the ordering of our outer actions. As esoteric students, we should try to manage our affairs so that they fit both with the affairs of others and with events around us. We should abstain from any behavior that would disturb others or otherwise go against what is happening around us. We should strive to direct our activity so that it integrates harmoniously into our surroundings, our situation in life, and so forth. When a situation prompts us to act, we should consider carefully how best to respond to this prompting. And when we act on our own initiative, we should weigh the consequences of what we intend to do as clearly as we can.

The fifth soul process comes into consideration at this point—namely, the arrangement and organization of our life as a whole. As esoteric students, we must strive to live in harmony with both nature and spirit. We must be neither overhasty nor slow and lazy. Hyperactivity and laxity should be equally alien to us. We should see life itself as a way of working and arrange it accordingly. We should take care of our health and regulate our habits so that a harmonious life is the result.

The sixth soul process has to do with human effort. As esoteric students we must assess our talents and abilities and then act in accordance with this self-knowledge. We should not try to do anything that is beyond our powers, yet we must always do whatever is within our powers to do. At the same time, we must set aspirations for ourselves that are connected to humanity's great ideals and obligations. We should not thoughtlessly place ourselves as mere cogs in the vast human machine, but try to understand our tasks and learn to look beyond our daily routines. Hence we should always strive to perfect the performance of our duties.

The seventh soul process involves the effort to learn as much as possible from life. As esoteric students, nothing comes to us in life that does not provide an opportunity to gather experiences useful for the future. Mistakes and imperfections become an incentive to perform more correctly and perfectly whenever a similar situation next arises. In the same way, we can learn from watching others. We should try to gather as rich a treasure of experience as possible, conscientiously drawing on it for advice at all times. We should do nothing without looking back upon the experiences that can help us to decide and act.

Finally, *the eighth soul process*: as esoteric students, we should periodically turn and look inward. We must sink, absorbed, into ourselves, gently taking counsel with ourselves, shaping and testing our basic principles of life, mentally reviewing what we know, weighing our obligations, pondering the meaning and purpose of life, and so forth.... The practice of these activities perfects our lotus flower, for the development of clairvoyance depends on such exercises. For example, the more our thoughts and words harmonize with events in the outer world, the more quickly we develop this gift. In contrast, when we think or say something untrue, we destroy something in the bud of the sixteen-petalled lotus flower. In this regard, truthfulness, sincerity, and honesty are constructive forces, while lying, falsity, and insincerity are destructive ones.

On the esoteric path, we must be aware that the important thing is not "good intentions," but what we actually do. If I think or say something that does not correspond to reality, I destroy something in my spiritual sense organ, regardless of how good I think my intentions are, just as a child will get burned by placing a hand in a fire, although acting out of ignorance.

To summarize, if we orient these soul processes as outlined here, the sixteen-petalled lotus flower will shine forth in glorious colors and move according to its inherent laws.

More on the eight petals

Certain forms of clairvoyant seeing appear as the result of distortions in the development of the lotus flower. In this case, the seeing is marked not only by illusions and fantastic ideas but also by deviance and instability in daily life. As a result of such warped development, a person may become fearful, jealous, conceited, arrogant, and so on—even though he or she did not have these traits before.

As stated above, eight of the sixteen petals of the lotus flower were developed in the far-distant past and reappear of their own accord during esoteric schooling. The care and attention of the student, therefore, must be directed toward developing the eight new petals. In false approaches to esoteric schooling, the already developed earlier petals can easily appear alone, while the new petals still needing to be formed remain stunted. This happens particularly when not enough attention is paid to logical, level-headed thinking in the training. Of prime importance is that the student of esotericism be a sensible person, devoted to clear thinking. Equally important is to strive for the greatest clarity in speech. When we begin to have a first inkling of the suprasensory, we are tempted to talk about it. But this only impedes our development. Until we have gained a certain degree of clarity in these matters, the less we say about them, the better.

At the beginning of our training, we may be surprised to find how little "curiosity" those who are spiritually schooled show for our experiences. Indeed, it would be healthiest for us if we said nothing about our experiences and spoke only about how well or how badly we managed to carry out the exercises or follow our instructions. Those who are schooled spiritually have sources other than a student's own direct account for evaluating his or her progress. Besides, talking about our experiences always somewhat hardens the eight petals we are developing—and these should remain soft and pliable.

The twelve-petalled lotus flower

THE TWELVE-PETALLED LOTUS FLOWER is formed as follows:

First, we pay attention to directing the sequence of our thoughts; this is the so-called "practice of controlling thoughts." Inwardly controlling our thinking processes develops the twelve-petalled flower, just as thinking true and meaningful thoughts develops the sixteen-petalled lotus flower. Thoughts that flit about like will-o'-the-wisps, following one another by chance and not in a logical, meaningful way, distort and damage the form of this flower. The more logically our thoughts follow one another, and the more we avoid all illogical thinking, the more perfectly this organ develops its proper form.

Therefore, whenever we hear an illogical thought, we should immediately allow the correct thought to pass through our mind. But, if we find ourselves in what seems to be an illogical environment, we should not withdraw in an unloving way for that reason, in order to further our development. By the same token, we should not feel an immediate urge to correct the illogicality we witness around us. Rather, we should inwardly and very quietly give the thoughts rushing at us from the outside a logical and meaningful direction. We should always strive to maintain this logical direction in our own thinking.

Second, we must bring an equally logical consistency into our actions; this is the practice of controlling our actions. Instability and disharmony in our actions injures the development of the twelve-petalled lotus flower. Thus, each of our actions should follow logically from whatever action came before. If we act today out of different principles than we did yesterday, we will never develop this lotus flower.

Third, we must cultivate perseverance. As long as we consider a goal we have set for ourselves to be correct and worthwhile, we should never let an outside influence deter us from striving to reach it. We should consider obstacles as challenges to be overcome, not as reasons for giving up.

Fourth, we must develop forbearance (or tolerance) toward other people, other beings, and events. We must suppress all unnecessary criticism of imperfection, evil, and wickedness and seek rather to understand everything that comes to meet us. Just as the sun does not withdraw its light from wickedness and evil, so we, too, should not withdraw our understanding and sympathy from anyone. When we meet adversity, we should not indulge in negative judgments but accept the inevitable and do our best to turn it to the good. Similarly, instead of considering the opinions of others only from our own standpoint, we should try to put ourselves into their position.

Fifth, we must develop openness and impartiality toward all the phenomena of life. This is sometimes called faith or trust. We must learn to approach every person and every being with trust. Such trust and confidence must inspire all our actions. We should never respond to something said to us with, "I don't believe that, because it contradicts the opinion I have already formed." When faced with something new, we must instead be willing to test our opinions and views and revise them if necessary. We must always remain receptive to whatever approaches us. We should trust in the effectiveness of whatever we undertake. All doubt and timidity should be banished from our being. If we have a goal, we must have faith in the power of our goal. Even a hundred failures should not be able to take this faith from us. This is the "faith that can move mountains."

Sixth, we must achieve a certain balance, or serenity, in life. As esoteric students, we should try to maintain an attitude of inner harmony, regardless of whether joy or sorrow comes to us. We should lose the habit of swinging between "up one minute and down the next." Instead, we should be as prepared to deal with misfortune and danger as with joy and good fortune.

The ten-petalled lotus flower

The development of THE TEN-PETALLED LOTUS FLOWER near the solar plexus requires cultivating soul care of a particularly subtle and delicate kind. Here it is a matter of learning to consciously control and master the sense impressions themselves. This is especially important in the early stages of clairvoyant seeing. Only by learning to control and master sense impressions can we avoid a source of countless illusions and arbitrary spiritual fantasies.

As a rule we do not realize what controls the occurrence of ideas and memories and how they are evoked. Consider the following: We are riding in a train, wrapped in our own thoughts, when suddenly our thinking takes a completely new turn; we remember something that happened many years ago and weave this into our present thoughts. What we do not notice is that our eyes, looking through the window, fell upon a person resembling someone involved in the event recalled. But we are unaware of what we saw. We are aware only of the effect it produced in us. Therefore we think that our memory of the event occurred "of its own accord."

How much in life comes about in this way! Many things play into our lives without our awareness of the connections. For example, we may dislike a certain color not knowing why; we have forgotten that a teacher, who tormented us years ago, used to wear a coat of that color. Countless illusions are based on such connections.

Many things are imprinted into the soul without also being assimilated into consciousness. For example, you read in the newspaper that a famous person died, and you believe—insist— that you had a "premonition" of this death the day before, although you saw and heard nothing that could have led to that thought. And it is true; as if spontaneously, the thought that this famous person would die arose in you the day before. But one fact escaped your notice; when you visited a friend a few hours before this thought arose, a newspaper was on the table. You did not read it, but unconsciously your eyes registered the headlines. They announced the critical condition of that celebrity, and you were unaware of this impression. The effect it produced, however, was your "premonition."

In the light of these examples, it is clear that such unconscious relationships present a great source of illusion and fantasy. The development of the ten-petalled lotus flower requires that we block this source. This lotus flower allows us to perceive deeply hidden soul qualities. But we cannot rely on the truth of these perceptions unless we are completely free of such deceptions. To achieve this, we must become masters of what affects us from the outer world. We must reach the point where we really do not receive impressions we don't want. Only a strong inner life can develop this capacity. It must actually enter our will and become second nature not to allow anything to affect us that we have not focused on intentionally. In other words, we must be completely unavailable to those impressions to which we have not turned our attention. We must see only what we want or will to see. What we do not turn our attention to in fact must not exist for us. The more lively and energetic our inner soul work becomes, the more we will achieve this. Students of esoteric training must avoid all mindless gazing and listening. Only the things that we deliberately focus our eyes and ears on should exist for us. We must make it a practice not to hear what we do not want to hear, regardless of the surrounding turmoil. Our eyes must become unreceptive to anything we do not choose to focus on. We must be surrounded as if by a kind of soul armor against all unconscious impressions.

This kind of strict self-discipline is the only way to develop the true form of the ten-petalled lotus flower. If we wish to pursue this path to higher knowledge and become true esoteric students, our soul life must become a life lived in a state of attention. We must know how to really keep away all that we do not want to pay attention to, or ought not to pay attention to. To this end, we turn our care and attention above all to our thought life. For example, we must choose a particular thought and then try to think through this thought only thinking such thoughts as we can integrate into it in full consciousness and complete freedom. If any random thoughts arise, we reject them; and if we link one thought with another, we consider carefully how this second thought arose. But this is only the beginning. For instance, if we feel a particular antipathy for something, we combat this feeling and try to develop a conscious relationship to the thing in question. As a result of these kinds of exercises, fewer and fewer unconscious elements interfere with our soul life.

To develop the six-petalled lotus flower

THE SIX-PETALLED LOTUS FLOWER located in the center of the body is even more difficult to develop. Its requires that we strive for the complete mastery of our whole being by becoming conscious of our self in such a way that, within this awareness, body, soul, and spirit are in perfect harmony. Physical activity, the inclinations and passions of the soul, and the thoughts and ideas of the spirit must be brought into perfect accord with one another. We should purify and ennoble the body to such an extent that our physical organs no longer compel us to do anything that is not in the service of our soul and spirit. The body should not urge upon our soul desires and passions that contradict pure and noble thinking. Nor should the spirit rule the soul with compulsory duties and laws like a slave driver. Rather, the soul should follow these obligations and laws of its own free inclination. As students we should not think of duties as something imposed upon us that we grudgingly perform; we should perform them because we love them.

This means that the soul must become free, poised in perfect balance between the senses and the spirit. We must reach the point in our development where we can surrender to our sense nature because it has been so purified that it no longer has the power to drag us down. We should no longer need to restrain our passions because these follow the right course on their own. Indeed, as long as we still need to mortify ourselves, we cannot advance beyond a certain level of esoteric training. Virtues that we have to force upon ourselves are without value.

As long as we still have cravings, they interfere with our training, even when we try not to give in to them. It makes no difference whether the desires arise from the body or the soul. For example, if we abstain from a certain stimulant to purify ourselves by denying ourselves the pleasure it affords, it does not help us unless the body is free of discomforts in the process. Such discomfort indicates only that the body still *craves* the stimulant—

and therefore abstaining is useless. In such cases, we may have to renounce our aspirations for the time being and wait for more favorable physical conditions—perhaps in a later life. In certain situations, a sensible renunciation is a much greater accomplishment than the continued striving for something that cannot be achieved under existing conditions. Such sensible renunciation advances our development more than the opposite course of persisting despite indications to the contrary.

The Six Essential Exercises

Following Steiner, who called them Nebenübungen ("side exercises"), these six exercises are called "subsidiary," or supplementary, because they should supplement or accompany whatever meditation path or practice we follow. They are essential and should be part of the life of every practitioner because they ensure that the "main," or central, practice (that they accompany) will be healthy. Steiner refers to them repeatedly, recommending them at all levels of inner work. One version, entitled "General Requirements for Anyone Wishing to Undertake Esoteric Schooling," was circulated as early as 1906. In other words, Steiner considered them foundational. Though sometimes spoken of in an offhand manner, they are really the keys to inner development. As such, they may also be thought of as "chakra" exercises.

A series of qualities

We must develop a series of qualities. To begin with, we must master our thoughts, particularly our train of thought. This is called *control of thoughts.* Just consider the way thoughts whirl about in our souls, how they flit like will-o'-the-wisps; one impression arises here, another there, and each changes our thinking. It is not true that we govern our thoughts; our thoughts govern us completely. We must reach the point where, at a given time in the day, we can become so absorbed in a thought that no other thought can enter and disturb our soul. In this way, we hold the reins of thought life for a while.

The second quality is to find a similar relationship to our actions, that is, to exercise *control over our actions.* Here it is necessary, occasionally at least, to act in ways that are not precipitated by anything external. Whatever is initiated by our place in life, our profession, or our situation does not lead more deeply into higher life. Higher life depends on such intimate matters as one's resolve to do something that springs completely from one's own initiative—even if it is something absolutely insignificant. No other actions contribute anything to the higher life.

The third quality to strive for is *equanimity*. People fluctuate back and forth between joy and sorrow. One moment they are beside themselves with joy, the next they are unbearably sad. Thus we allow ourselves to be rocked on the waves of life, on joy or sorrow. We must reach equanimity and steadiness. Neither the greatest sorrow nor the greatest joy must disturb one's composure. One must become steadfast and even-tempered.

The fourth soul quality is to *understand every being*. Nothing expresses more beautifully what it means to understand every being than the legend passed down to us, not by the Gospel, but by a Persian story. Jesus was crossing a field with his disciples, and as they went along, they encountered the decaying corpse of a dog. It looked horrible. Jesus stopped and looked at it with admiration, saying, "What beautiful teeth this animal has!" Within the ugly, Jesus found an element of beauty. Try always to approach what is wonderful in every phenomenon of outer reality. You will see that everything contains an aspect that can be affirmed. Do as Christ did when he admired the beautiful teeth of the dead dog. Practicing this will lead you to a great ability to tolerate anything, and you will gain an understanding of everything and of every being.

The fifth quality is *complete openness* toward everything new that meets us. Most people judge new things according the old things they already know. If someone comes and tells them something new, they immediately respond with an opposite opinion. But we must not confront a new communication immediately with our own opinion. We must instead always remain alert for the possibility of learning something new. We can learn, even from a small child. Even if you were the wisest person, you should be willing to hold back your own judgment and listen to others. We must develop this ability to listen, because it enables us to encounter matters with the greatest possible openness. In esotericism, this is called "faith." It is the power not to oppose, which weakens the impression made by the new.

The sixth quality is something we all receive after we have developed the first five. This is *inner harmony*. Those who have the other qualities are also inwardly harmonious. Furthermore, it is necessary for those seeking spiritual development to strengthen their *feeling for freedom* to the greatest degree. A feeling for freedom enables us to look within ourselves for the center of our being and to stand on our own two feet, so that we do not have to ask everyone what we should do. Thus, we can stand upright and act freely. This also is a quality that one needs to acquire.

Once we develop these inner qualities, we stand above all the dangers that can arise from the division in human nature. The qualities of our lower nature can no longer affect us. We can no longer stray from the path. These qualities, therefore, must be formed with the greatest precision. Then we enter the esoteric life.

—Berlin, December 7, 1905

The six exercises from the point of view of rhythm

There is a universal cosmic rule we must never forget: *rhythm restores power*. This is a fundamental esoteric principle. Most people today live their lives completely devoid of any regular rhythm, especially in their thinking and behavior. Those who allow the distractions of the outer world to take hold cannot avoid the dangers to the physical body during esoteric development, because the forces of renewal are withdrawn. Consequently, we must work to introduce a rhythmic element into life. Naturally, we cannot arrange our days so that each day is exactly the same. But we can at least pursue some activities regularly. Indeed, this is necessary for anyone who wants to develop on the esoteric path. For example, we should do certain meditation and concentration exercises at a deliberate time every morning. We can also bring rhythm into our lives if every evening we review the events of the day in reverse order. The more regularities we can introduce, so much the better. In this way, life exists in harmony with the laws of the world. Everything in the system of nature is rhythmic—the sun's course, the seasons, day and night, and so on. Plants, too, grow rhythmically. True, the higher we go in the kingdoms of nature, the less rhythm we find, but even in animals we can observe a certain degree of rhythm—for example, they mate according to regular cycles. Only human beings lead a chaotic life with no rhythm; nature has deserted it.

Our task, therefore, is to deliberately infuse some rhythm into this chaotic life. And we have certain means available to us through which we can bring harmony and rhythm into our physical and etheric bodies. Both bodies then gradually develop rhythms that will self-regulate when the astral body withdraws. When they are forced out of their proper rhythm during the day, they will, on their own, regain the right kind of movement while at rest. The means to do this involve the following exercises. These practices must be done in addition to meditation:

I. *Thought control.* This means that, at least for a short time each day, you stop all sorts of thoughts from drifting through your mind. For a space of time, you allow peace and tranquillity to enter your thinking. You think a definite idea, place it in the center of your thinking, and logically arrange your thoughts so that they are all closely related to the original idea. If you do this even for only a minute, it can be very important for the rhythm of the physical and etheric bodies.

2. *Initiative in action.* You must perform some action, however trivial, that originates with your own initiative. This is some task you

have assigned yourself. Most actions are a response to family circumstances, education, vocation, and so on. Consider how little arises as the result of your own initiative. Consequently, you must spend a little time performing acts derived only from you. They need not be important; very insignificant actions accomplish the same purpose.

3. *Detachment, imperturbability.* You must learn to regulate your emotions so that you are not up in the sky one moment and down in the dumps the next. Those who refuse to do this for fear of losing their unconventional nature or artistic sensibility can never develop esoterically. Detachment, or imperturbability, means that you master yourself throughout the greatest joys and the deepest grief. Indeed, we become truly receptive to the world's joys and sorrows only when we do not enter them egotistically. The greatest artists owe their great achievements precisely to this detachment, because, through it, they opened their eyes to the subtle, inwardly significant impressions.

4. *Impartiality or freedom from prejudice.* This quality sees goodness in everything and looks for the positive element everywhere....

5. *Faith.* In the esoteric sense, faith implies something rather different than what it usually means. During esoteric development, you must never allow your assessment of the future to be influenced by the past. In esoteric development you must exclude all that you have experienced thus far, so that you can meet each new experience with new faith. The esotericist must do this quite consciously. For instance, if someone comes to you and says that the church steeple is leaning at a forty-five degree angle, most people would say that this is not possible. Esotericists must always allow for the possibility of belief. They must go so far as to have faith in everything that happens in the world; otherwise, they block their way to new experiences. You must always remain open to new experiences. In this way, your

physical and etheric bodies will assume a condition that may be likened to the contented mood of a setting hen.

6. *Inner Balance.* Inner balance is a natural result of the other five qualities; it is formed gradually from the other five qualities. You must keep these six qualities in mind, grasp life, and progress gradually—like drops of water wearing away a stone in the proverb.

—Stuttgart, September 2–5, 1906

Qualities needed for attaining higher knowledge

There are certain qualities that should acquired through practice by those who want to find the way into the higher world. Before all else, these emphasize the soul's mastery over its train of thought, its will, and its feelings. The method for bringing about such mastery through practice has two goals. First, the practice is meant to imbue the soul with stability, certainty, and equilibrium to the extent that it retains these qualities even when a second "I" is born out of it. Second, it is meant to give this second "I" strength and support for its journey.

What our *thinking* needs most of all for spiritual training is *objectivity*. In this regard, life is the great teacher of the "I" in the physical world. If the soul chose to allow its thoughts to wander aimlessly, life would immediately correct. It would not allow our thinking to come into conflict with life. The soul's thinking must correspond to the actual course of life's realities. When we turn our attention away from the physical world of the senses, we are no longer subject to its automatic correction. Our thinking will go astray if it is not able to self-correct. This is why students of the spirit must train their thinking so that it can set its own direction and goals. Their thinking must teach itself inner stability and the ability to stick strictly to one subject. For this reason, the appropriate "thought exercises" we undertake should not deal with unfamiliar and complicated objects, but with ones that are simple and familiar.

Over a matter of months, if we can overcome ourselves to the point of being able to focus our thoughts for at least five minutes a day on some ordinary object (for example, a pin, a pencil, or the like), and if, during this time, we exclude all thoughts unrelated to this object, we will have made a big step in the right direction. (We can consider a new object each day or stay with the same one for several days.) Even those who consider themselves thinkers because of their scientific education should not scorn this means of preparing themselves for spiritual training, because if we fix our thoughts on something very familiar for a certain period of time, we can be certain that we are thinking objectively. If we ask, What is a pencil made of? How are these materials prepared? How are they put together to make pencils? When were pencils invented? and so on, our thoughts correspond to reality much more closely than they do if we think about the origin of human beings or the nature of life. *Simple thought exercises are better for developing objective thinking about the Saturn, Sun, and Moon phases of evolution than any complicated scholarly ideas,* because what we think about is not the point, at least initially. The point is to think objectively, using our own inner strength. Once we have taught ourselves objectivity by practicing on sense-perceptible physical processes that are easily surveyed, our thinking becomes accustomed to striving for objectivity even when it does not feel constrained by the physical world of the senses and its laws. We break ourselves of the habit of allowing our thoughts to wander without regard for the facts.

The soul must become a ruler in the domain of the *will* just as it is in the world of thoughts. Here again, life itself appears as the controlling element in the physical world of the senses. It makes us need certain things, and our will feels roused to satisfy these needs. For the sake of higher training, we must get used to strictly obeying our own commands. If we do this, we will become less

and less inclined to desire nonessentials. Dissatisfaction and instability in our life of will, however, are based on desiring things
without having any clear concept of realizing these desires. This
dissatisfaction can disrupt our entire mental life when a higher
"I" is trying to emerge from the soul.

A good exercise is to tell ourselves to do something daily at a
specific time, over a number of months: Today, at this particular
time, I will do *this*. We then gradually become able to determine
what to do and when to do it in a way that makes it possible to
carry out the action in question with great precision. In this way,
we rise above damaging thoughts, such as: "I'd like this, I want to
do that," which disregard totally the feasibility of what we want.
In *Faust*, Goethe put these words into the mouth of his seeress,
Manto: "I love whomever longs for the impossible." Goethe himself said, "Living in ideas means treating the impossible as if it
were possible." These statements, however, should not be used as
objections to what has been presented here, because what Goethe
and his seeress Manto ask can be accomplished only by those who
have trained themselves in desiring what is possible in order to
then be able to apply their strong will to "impossibilities" in a
way that transforms them into possibilities.

For the sake of spiritual training, the soul should also acquire a
certain degree of *composure with regard to the domain of feeling*. For this to
happen, the soul must master its expressions of joy and sorrow,
pleasure and pain. Many prejudices become evident with regard to
acquiring this particular quality. We might imagine that we would
become dull and unreceptive to the world around us if we could
not empathize with rejoicing or pain. However, that is not the
point. The soul should rejoice when there is reason to rejoice, and
should feel pain when something sad happens. It is only meant to
master its *expressions* of joy and sorrow, of pleasure and displeasure.
With this as our goal, we will soon notice that rather than becoming dulled to pleasurable and painful events in our surroundings,
the opposite is true. We are becoming more receptive to these

things than we were previously. Admittedly, acquiring this character trait requires strict self-observation over a long period of time.
We must make sure that we are able to empathize fully with joy
and sorrow without losing ourselves and expressing our feelings
involuntarily. What we are meant to suppress is not our justified
pain, but involuntary weeping; not our abhorrence of a misdeed,
but blind rage; not alertness to danger, but fruitless fear; and so on.

Exercises like this are the only way for students of the spirit to
acquire the mental tranquillity that is needed to prevent the soul
from leading a second, unhealthy life, like a shadowy double,
alongside the higher "I" when this "I" is born and especially when
it begins to be active. Especially with regard to these things, it is
important not to succumb to self-deception. It can easily seem to
people that they already possess a certain equilibrium in ordinary
life and that they therefore do not need this exercise, but in fact it
is doubly necessary for people like this. It's quite possible to be
calm and composed in confronting things in ordinary life and yet
have our suppressed lack of equilibrium assert itself all the more
when we ascend into a higher world. It is essential to realize that
for purposes of spiritual training, what we seem to possess already
is much less important than systematically practicing what we
need to acquire. This sentence is quite correct, regardless of how
contradictory it may seem. No matter what life may have taught
us, *what we teach ourselves* is what serves the purposes of spiritual
training. If life has taught us excitability we need to break that
habit, but if it has taught us complacency we need to shake ourselves up through self-education so that our souls' reactions correspond to the impressions they receive. People who cannot laugh
at anything have as little control over their lives as people who are
constantly provoked to uncontrollable laughter.

An additional way of training our thinking and feeling is by
acquiring a quality we can call "positivity." ...The erroneous, the
bad, and the ugly must not prevent the soul from finding the true,
the good, and the beautiful wherever they are present. We must not

confuse this positivity with being artificially uncritical or arbitrarily closing our eyes to things that are bad, false, or inferior. It is possible to admire a dead animal's "beautiful teeth" and still see the decaying corpse; the corpse does not prevent us from seeing the beautiful teeth. We cannot consider bad things good and false things true, but we can reach the point where the bad does not prevent us from seeing the good and errors do not keep us from seeing the truth.

Our thinking undergoes a certain maturing process in connection with the will when we attempt never to allow anything we have experienced to deprive us of our unbiased receptivity to new experiences. For students of the spirit, the thought, "I've never heard of that; I don't believe it," should totally lose its meaning. During specific periods of time, we should be intent on using every opportunity to learn something new concerning every thing and every being. If we are ready and willing to take previously unaccustomed points of view, we can learn from every current of air, every leaf, every babbling baby. Admittedly, it is easy to go too far with regard to this ability. At any given stage in life, we should not disregard all our previous experiences. We should indeed judge what we are experiencing in the present on the basis of past experiences. This belongs on one side of the scales; on the other, however, students of the spirit must place their inclination to constantly experience new things and especially their faith in the possibility that new experiences will contradict old ones.

We have now listed five soul qualities that students in a genuine spiritual training need to acquire: control of one's train of thought, control of one's will impulses, composure in the face of joy and sorrow, positivity in judging the world, and receptivity in one's attitude toward life. Having spent certain periods of time practicing these qualities consecutively, we will then need to bring them into harmony with each other in our souls. We will need to practice them in pairs, or in combinations of three and one at the same time, and so on, in order to bring about this harmony.

—From *An Outline of Esoteric Science*

The Backward Review, or "Retrospect"

Another central, basic, and indispensable practice is the Rückshau (literally "backward look" or "look back"). As the last activity each night, one goes over the events of the day, starting from the last thing one did and moving backward from that to the first thing in the morning. In principle, and after much practice, however, one need not stop there. One can continue back—over the previous days, months, and even years. In fact, there is no end to how far back one might go.

IN THE EVENING

In the evening, before going to sleep, we should direct our thoughts back over the day's events. It is not a matter of recalling in our souls as many of the day's experiences as possible, but only the most important.

We ask ourselves what we can learn from our experiences or activities. In this way, life becomes an object lesson. We face ourselves so that every day we learn something for daily life. Thereby, too, we take the past with us into the future and prepare the way for our immortality.

—Letter, January 1905

PERCEPTION NEEDED FOR THE ASTRAL PLANE

The review must be done from the present to the past—from the present backward. This accustoms us to the kind of perception we need for the astral plane.

—Esoteric Hour, June 6, 1907

DIRECT VISION

In the backward review, when we translate ourselves into what we have experienced, we should do this in such a way that we experience the difference between the soul experience [of the backward review] and the actual experience in the outer world. This is like the difference between observing a landscape with one's eyes closed as a memory, and looking at it with open eyes and a direct view. It is the same as the relationship between memory and the backward review. (Here, memory is remembering, whereas the backward review is viewing.)

For an initiate, memory gradually disappears and direct vision of what one wants to remember replaces it.

One must create an image of one's daily experience, precisely and clearly in every detail—clothing, faces—and then look at the event in the image—*how* something was spoken, done, and so forth. It is very important to recall to mind little experiences that are not so interesting and that require effort to remember, because this stimulates our inner forces. The ability to create images forms the power of imagination. It is not a matter of how complete the experiences are, but the clarity of the images. Not a muscle should be strained in doing this work.

IMAGES

[The evening review] must be done backward to accustom us to the way of perception on the astral plane. One must try to make everything possible in images. In the beginning, if you have had eighty significant experiences, you do not need to recall all eighty before the soul as images; you must choose. Finally, the whole day will unroll as in a tableau. Again, it has much more to do with small unimportant actions, for it is the effort that awakens the powers of the soul.

REVERSE ORDER

Being able to look at our experiences, joys, and sorrows as if they belonged to someone else is a good preparation for spiritual training. We can gradually gain this ability by taking time after work each day to allow images of the day's experiences to pass before us in spirit. We should see ourselves in images within these experiences. In other words, we must look in on ourselves in our daily lives as if from outside. We can gain an aptitude for this kind of self-observation if we begin by visualizing small isolated portions of our daily lives. With practice, we become increasingly skillful in this retrospective view, and after considerable repetition, we can quickly form a complete picture.

Looking at experiences in reverse order is especially valuable for spiritual training, because it forces us to free our visualizations from our usual habit of merely tracing the course of sense-perceptible events with our thinking. In *reversed thinking,* we visualize things correctly, but we are not limited by their sense-perceptible sequence. This is something we need if we are to find our way into the spiritual world. Our ability to visualize is strengthened in a healthy way. This is why, in addition to visualizing our daily lives in reverse, it is also beneficial to practice this with other things, such as the sequence of a drama, a narrative, a melody, and so on.

—*An Outline of Esoteric Science*

LOVE AND THE BACKWARD REVIEW

The third step to higher knowledge—needed for rising to intuition—must be achieved by perfecting a faculty that our materialistic age does not recognize as a cognitive power. What is shown through intuition is revealed only when we develop and spiritualize our capacity for *love.* We must be able to make the capacity for love into a cognitive force. A good preparation for this is to free ourselves from unnecessary dependence on external things. We can do this, for example, by making it a regular practice to picture our past experiences not in their normal order but in reverse.

In ordinary thinking, we slavishly accept the sequence of world events. We maintain the earlier as the earlier and the later as the later. Watching a play, we view the first act first, then the second, and so on. But if we can accustom ourselves by picturing it all by beginning at the end and going backward through the acts—fifth, fourth, third and so on—we can break from the ordinary sequence. We go backward instead of forward.... Thus we free the soul's inner activity from its habits. And when we do so, our inner soul and spirit experiences gradually reach a point *where soul and spirit break from the physical and etheric elements.*

Every evening, we can prepare for this breaking away by practicing a backward review of our day's experiences, beginning with the last event and moving backward. Whenever possible, even the details should be conceived in a backward direction. If you went upstairs, picture yourself first on the top step, then on the step below, and so on, back to the bottom.

You will probably object that the day is so long and full of experiences. First, try taking episodes—picturing, for example, going up and downstairs in reverse. This will give you inner flexibility, so that, in three or four minutes, you will gradually be able to go back in imagination through a whole day.

—Lecture, August 20, 1923

Living the Year Spiritually

Rhythm and repetition are the heart of spiritual life, as they are of all life. From the tiniest, innermost parts of our bodies through the heavenly bodies of our solar system and galaxy to the very limits of the conceivable universe, we are surrounded everywhere by rhythms.

No wonder, then, that for Plato and the ancients the height of wisdom and harmony was to attune the soul to the universal rhythmic nature. Doing so, we order our lives, which is truly the "first step" in inner development. This involves more than order.

Since we are cognitive beings, the order and rhythm we come to know become sources of knowledge. By repeating the same meditation, for instance, we learn how it is different every time. The more we keep everything the same, the more the difference appears. And not just difference—for this "difference" teaches us both about the spiritual world ("grace") and our own contribution in interaction with it.

For this reason, Rudolf Steiner gave many exercises and meditations to be done on a daily, weekly, or monthly rhythm.

Five daily meditations

I

(morning)   In the world's divinity
In the world's spirit
In the world's soul
I will seek myself
I will find myself
I know

(evening) I know
I will find myself
Because I will seek myself
In the world's soul
In the world's spirit
In the world's divinity

II

(morning) May my soul bloom
In love for all existence
May my spirit live
In the soul of being
May my self rest
In the world's divinity
So will I be

(evening) I will stir myself
To be in the world's divinity
May my self rest within it
May my spirit live
In the soul of being
May my soul bloom
In love for all existence
Wisdom in spirit

III

(morning) In the world's divinity
In the world's spirit
In the world's soul
I will find myself
To rest in it
To live in it
To be in it

(*evening*)

I will be
I will live
I will rest
I will find myself
In the world's soul
In the world's spirit
In the world's divinity

IV

(*morning*)

Steadfast, I place myself in existence [left foot]
Certain, I step into life's way [right foot]
Loving, I maintain in being's core [left hand]
Hoping, I engage all doing [right hand]
Peace leads me to the goal [heart]
Peace leads me into existence [heart]
Wisdom, I seek in all thinking [head]

(*evening*)

Wisdom, I seek in all thinking [head]
Peace leads me into existence [heart]
Peace leads me to the goal [heart]
Hoping, I engage all doing [right hand]
Loving, I maintain my being's core [left hand]
Certain, I step into life's way [right foot]
Steadfast, I place myself in existence [left foot]

—From 1907 on

V

(*evening*)

Pure rays of light
Show me the world's spirit
The pure warmth of love
Shows me the world's soul
Divine intimacy
In my heart
In my soul

(morning) In my soul
In my heart
Divine intimacy
Show me the world's soul
The pure warmth of love
Shows me the world's spirit
The light's pure rays

—February 1912

Six-monthly exercise

These six basic exercises are recommended as a six-month program.

1. *The first requirement is to acquire completely clear thinking.* To achieve this goal, you must—if only for a short time everyday, say five minutes, but the more the better—free yourself of the thoughts that flit through your mind like will-o'-the-wisps. You must become the master of your thought world. You are not the master when outer circumstances—job, tradition, social relations, nationality, time of day, certain activities, and so on—determine what you think and how you elaborate it. Therefore, during the time you set aside, *of your own free will* you must empty your soul of the ordinary daily flow of thoughts and *through your own initiative* move a single thought to the center of your soul. Do not think that it has to be a particularly striking or interesting thought. It is much better for what you are seeking in esoteric development to begin first with an uninteresting or insignificant thought. You will then more easily arouse the *autonomous powers* of thinking itself, which is essential. When you start with a "thought" that is already interesting, it carries thinking with it. It is better to do this exercise using a pin as the object of meditation than

to try to do it on the life of Napoleon. Starting on your own initiative with such a thought—the pin—associate it with everything that you can find related to it. At the end of your meditation, your thought should be just as colorful and living as it was at the beginning....

2. When this exercise has been practiced for about a month, a second may be added. *Think of an action that you would certainly not perform in ordinary circumstances; make it your duty to do it every day.* It is best to choose an action that will take the longest time to do. Again, it is better to start with an inconsequential action that you must, as it were, compel yourself to perform. For example, buy a plant and water it at the same time each day. After a certain time, another similar activity may be added to the first, and later a third, and so on, as long as they are compatible with carrying out your other responsibilities. This exercise should again last a whole month. As much as possible, during the second month the first exercise should be continued....

3. During the third month, a new exercise should be placed at the center of life; equanimity is developed in relation to life's fluctuations of joy and sorrow, pleasure and pain. Inner harmony must consciously replace mood swings from the heights of jubilation to the depths of despair. Be careful not to get carried away by pleasure or knocked down by pain. No experience should lead you to uncontrollable anger or irritation; no expectation should lead to anxiety or fear; no situation should disturb your composure; and so on. Do not be afraid that this exercise will make your life dry or impoverished. Rather, you will quickly notice that the experiences to which this exercise is applied are replaced by purer soul qualities. If you are

attentive to subtlety, you will notice one day that inner
peace pervades your body....

4. In the fourth month, as a new exercise, practice
   "positivity." This involves always looking for goodness, the
   excellence, beauty, and so on in every event, being, and
   thing.... If you turn your mind consciously toward the
   positive in every experience, you will gradually notice a
   feeling creeping into you, as if your whole skin were
   becoming porous. It is as if your soul were opening to all
   kinds of secret and delicate processes that had escaped
   your notice. It is most important to overcome lack of
   attentiveness to these subtle things. Once it has been
   noticed that this feeling expresses itself in the soul as a
   kind of bliss, you should try, in thought, to guide this
   feeling to the heart, and from there let it flow into the eyes,
   and then into the space all around you. You will notice
   that you thus acquire an intimate relationship with this
   space. You grow out and beyond yourself, as it were. You
   learn to regard this space as part of you....

5. In the fifth month, try to develop the feeling of meeting
   every new experience with complete openness.... At every
   moment, be ready to encounter and accept completely
   new experiences.... If you pay attention to this attitude,
   you will notice something coming to life in the space
   around you. This experience is extremely delicate and
   subtle. You must make an effort to be attentive to this
   delicate vibration in the environment, allowing it to flow
   as it were through all the five senses, especially the eyes,
   ears, and skin, insofar as the latter contains the sense of
   warmth....

6. In the sixth month, repeat all five exercises systematically,
   alternating them regularly.

Exercises for the days of the week

We usually perform certain soul processes without care or attention. There are eight of these to which we must now begin to give close attention to and care for: *Thinking – Judging – Speaking – Doing – Organizing – Caring – Remembering – Examining.*

Naturally, it is best to begin by undertaking *only one process or exercise at a time*—for example, the first exercise for one or two weeks, then the second, and so on, until beginning again. The eighth—*right meditation*—is best done daily. This will help us gradually attain true self-knowledge as well as monitor our progress.

After we have gone through the whole sequence of exercises in this way, we may then, beginning with Saturday, practice the sequence for about five minutes on a daily and weekly basis.

SATURDAY : RIGHT THINKING

Be aware of your *thoughts*. Think only meaningful thoughts. Gradually learn to separate in your thoughts the essential from the nonessential, the eternal from the transitory, and truth from mere opinion. When listening to conversation, try to become inwardly still, renouncing all agreement and, more important, all negative judgments (criticism and rejection). Do this in both thought and feeling. This is "right thinking."

SUNDAY : RIGHT JUDGMENT

Decide on even the most insignificant issues only after full, well-founded deliberation and reflection. All unthinking behavior and all meaningless actions should be discarded from the soul. Our reasons for everything we do should be fully deliberated. We should abstain from doing anything that has no significant reason. Once we are convinced that a decision is correct, we should adhere to it with inner steadfastness. This is "right judgment," because it was made independently of attraction or aversion.

MONDAY : RIGHT WORD

Only serious, meaningful speech must leave the lips of those who strive for higher development. All talk for the sake of talking—to pass the time, for example—is harmful. Avoid the usual sort of conversation that involves jumbled, simultaneous crosstalk. This does not mean that you should cut yourself off from interacting with others. Especially in such interactions, your speech should gradually become increasingly meaningful. Listen thoughtfully to every statement and answer. Consider every approach. Never speak without a reason. Prefer silence. Try not to talk too much or too little. Listen quietly and process what you hear. This exercise may be called "right word."

TUESDAY : RIGHT DEED

Our outer actions should not disturb others. When you are moved inwardly (by conscience) to act, carefully weigh how best to employ the occasion for the good of the whole, and the happiness of others and the eternal. When you act from yourself and your own initiative, weigh the consequences of your actions in the most fundamental way. This is called "right deed."

WEDNESDAY : RIGHT STANDPOINT

In ordering your life, live in harmony with nature and spirit. Do not get buried in the external knickknacks of life. Avoid all that brings restlessness and haste to your life. Be neither impetuous nor lazy. Consider life as a means of inner work and development and act accordingly. One may speak, in this context, of "right standpoint."

THURSDAY : RIGHT STRIVING

In human striving, take care not to do anything beyond your power. At the same time, however, do not leave anything undone that is within your ability. Look beyond the moment, the ordinary, and pose goals (ideals) for yourself that are connected with the highest of human responsibilities. In relation to these exercises, for example, try to develop yourself so that later—if not immediately—you may be better able to help and advise others. All this may be summed in this way: "Let all the preceding exercises become a habit."

FRIDAY : RIGHT MEMORY

Strive to learn as much as possible from life. Nothing happens that does not give us the opportunity to gather experiences that are useful for life. If you have done something incorrectly or incompletely, it becomes an opportunity to do it correctly or completely later on. When you see others act, observe them with the same end in mind (but not without love). Do nothing without looking at past experiences that may help in your decisions and actions. If you are attentive, you can learn much from everyone, including small children. This exercise may be called "right memory," or recalling what you have learned from your experiences.

SUMMARY : RIGHT MEDITATION

From time to time, turn your gaze inward, even if for only five minutes at the same time each day. You should sink into yourself; take careful counsel with yourself; test and form your principles of life. In your mind, go through your insights—or the opposite. Weigh your duties. Consider the substance and the real goals of your life. Experience serious displeasure at your faults and imperfections. In other words, try to discover what is essential and permanent, and earnestly propose the appropriate goals—for instance, the virtues you should acquire. Do not make the mistake of thinking you have done something well; always strive harder, instead, toward the highest standards. This exercise is called "right mediation."

Other sequences

I

MONTHLY SEQUENCE

Month 1:   Self-confidence (faith and trust in oneself)
Month 2:   Self-control (self-rule)
Month 3   Perseverance

II

WEEKLY SEQUENCE

Week 1: How do I attain self-confidence?
Week 2: How do I attain self-control?
Week 3: How do I attain presence of mind?

—December 1906

III

SEVEN-WEEK EXERCISE

1. I understand the world.
2. I know what was before the world.
3. I break through into divine being—love shines.
4. I grasp divine being—love conceives.
5. Divine being streams into me.
6. Love fills me completely.

Each sentence is to be practiced for a week.
In the seventh week, practice all six together.

—c. 1923

The seven moods: planetary meditations for the days of the week

Expressing the Time-Being of the Hierarchies

Writing to an early student, Steiner wrote of "seven verses distributed over the seven days of the week. You practice them by meditating Friday for Saturday, Saturday for Sunday, and so on. [In an occult sense, the day begins at 6 p.m.] You can do this more than once in a day. Try for twenty or thirty minutes to exhaust the depths of a given verse. By doing this, you will gain much in connection with the mystery of the all-penetrating sevenfoldness."

♄

Friday Evening for Saturday : Saturn

Great encompassing Spirit,
Who filled infinite space
When of my bodily members
None was yet present:
You were.
I lift up my soul to you.
I was in you.
I was a part of your force.
You sent forth your forces
And the Earth's primal beginning
Mirrored the first archetype
Of my bodily form.
In your forces sent forth
I myself was.
You were.
My archetype beheld you.
It gazed on me,
I, who was a part of you.
You were.

SATURDAY FOR SUNDAY : SUN

Great encompassing Spirit,
    Many archetypes sprang from your life
    When my life forces
    Were not yet present.
You were.
    I raise my soul to you.
    I was in you.
    I was a part of your forces.
    You united
    With the Earth's primal beginning
    With the living Sun
    And gave me the force of life.
In your radiating life forces
    I myself was.
You were.
    My life force radiated in yours
    In space.
My body began its becoming
    In time.
You were.

☾

SUNDAY FOR MONDAY : MOON

Great encompassing Spirit,
    Perceptive feeling sensation shone in your life forms
When my sensation
    Was not yet present.
You were.
    I raise my soul to you.
I was in you.

I was a part of your perceptive feeling sensations.
You united
　　With the Earth's primal beginning
　　And in my body
　　My own perceptive feeling sensations
　　Began to shine.
In your feelings
　　I felt myself.
You were.
　　My perceptive feeling sensations felt your being in themselves.
　　My soul began to be in herself
　　Because you were in me.
You were.

MONDAY FOR TUESDAY : MARS

Great encompassing Spirit,
　　Cognition lived in your perceptive feeling sensations
　　When cognition was not yet given to me.
You were.
　　I raise my soul to you.
I drew into my body.
　　I lived in my perceptive feeling sensations.
You were in the living Sun.
　　In my perceptive feeling sensation
　　Your being lived as my being.
My soul life
　　Was outside your life.
You were.
My soul felt her being in herself.
　　Yearning arose in her.
　　The yearning for you
　　Out of whom she came.
You were.

Tuesday for Wednesday : Mercury

Great encompassing Spirit,
    In cognition of your being is world cognition
Which will come to me.
You are.
    I will unite my soul with you.
May your cognizing leader
    Light my path.
    Feeling your leader
    I pass through the path of life.
Your leader is in the living Sun.
    He lives in my yearning.
    I will take up his being
    In mine.
You are.
    May my force take up
    The leader's force in itself.
    Blessedness draws into me.
    The blessedness in which the soul
    Finds the spirit.
You are.

Wednesday for Thursday : Jupiter

Great encompassing Spirit,
    The Earth's life streams in your light,
    My life is in yours.
You are.
    My soul acts in yours.
With your leader I go my way.
    I live with him.

His being is an image
Of my own being.
You are.
The leader's being within my soul
Finds you, encompassing Spirit.
Blessedness is mine
From your being's breath.
You are.

THURSDAY FOR FRIDAY : VENUS

Great encompassing Spirit,
I live in your life with the life of the Earth.
In you I am.
You are.
I am in you.
The leader has brought me to you
I live in you.
Your spirit is
My own being's image.
You are.
Spirit has found
The encompassing spirit.
Divine blessedness walks onward
To new world creation.
You are. I am. You are.

✳

AFTER EACH OF THE ABOVE :

Great encompassing Spirit,
I raise my "I" up from below
May it be capable of intuiting you encompassing all.

May my being's spirit be illuminated
  With your messengers' light,
May my being's soul be kindled
  By the fiery flames of your servants,
May the will of my "I" grasp
  The force of your Creator Word.
You are.
  May your Light stream into my spirit,
  May your Life warm my soul,
  May your Being penetrate my will
  So that understanding may seize my "I"
  For the burning of your Light,
  For the love warmth of your Life,
  For the Creator-Word of your Being.
You are.

The twelve moods: zodiacal meditations

These verses were written in 1915 for the first group of eurythmists, after
they had completed their basic training. Each mood expresses an aspect of
"the twelvefold quality that exists in the universe as the Zodiac," as well as
"the sevenfoldness that exists as the planetary sequence." Thus there are
twelve verses—for Aries, Taurus, Gemini, Cancer, Leo, Virgo, Libra, Scor-
pio, Sagittarius, Capricorn, Aquarius, and Pisces—each of which contains
seven lines that express the seven planetary beings: Sun, Venus, Mercury
Mars, Jupiter, Saturn, and Moon. Introducing the first performance of these
moods, Steiner said, "This has nothing to do with imitating modern astrolo-
gers, whose methods surpass all materialism, simply adding ignorant
superstition to materialist ignorance. Rather, we are concerned here with
introducing the lawful relationships of a spiritual world that manifest
equally in the universe and in the human being. True spiritual science does
not try to find human laws from the constellations of the stars, but to find
both human and natural laws from the spiritual world."

ARIES

Arise, blazing light,
Seize the being of becoming,
Take hold of the forces' weaving,
Ray yourself out, awakening essence.
Overcome resistance,
Disappear in time's stream.
O blazing light, stay!

TAURUS

Grow bright, essential brilliance,
Feel the power of becoming,
Weave together life's threads
In real worlds' being,
In ingenious revelation,
In shining realization of being.
O essential brilliance, grow bright!

GEMINI

Disclose yourself, solar being,
Induce to movement the urge to rest,
Embrace the desire to strive
For the mighty reign of life,
For blessed comprehension of life,
For the fruitful ripening of becoming.
O solar being, persist!

♋

CANCER

You resting shining brilliance,
Engender life's warmth,
Warm soul life,
To prove itself forcefully,
To penetrate itself spiritually,
In restful light production.
Shining brilliance, grow strong!

♌

LEO

Stream through with senses' force
Feeling community of essence,
The finished being of the worlds,
For the willing decision to be.
In the streaming blaze of life,
In the presiding pain of becoming,
With senses' force, arise!

♍

VIRGO

Behold the worlds, O soul!
May the soul grasp the worlds,
May the spirit take hold of essence,
Work out of life's powers,
Build in will's experience,
Trust in the worlds' blossoming,
O soul, cognize the essences!

♎

LIBRA

The worlds uphold the worlds,
Essence experiences itself in essence,
Being surrounds being.
And essence produces essence
For the evolving pouring forth of deeds,
In peaceful world enjoyment.
O worlds, bear the worlds!

SCORPIO

Being consumes beings
Yet being halts in beings.
In activity becoming disappears,
In becoming activity holds still.
In the punishing rule of the worlds,
In avenging self-forming,
Essence sustains the beings.

♐

SAGITTARIUS

Becoming attains the power of being.
The power of becoming dies into what is.
What is attained resolves striving's desire
In the rule of life's power of will.
In dying the rule of worlds ripens,
Forms disappear in forms.
May what is feel what is!

CAPRICORN

May what is to come rest on what is past.
May what is past feel what is to come
For powerful present being.
In inner resistance to life
May the power of the worlds' being grow strong,
May life's power to act blossom forth.
May the past bear what is to come!

AQUARIUS

May what is bounded sacrifice itself to the boundless.
May what misses boundaries find
Its own boundaries in the depths.
May it raise itself in the stream,
Enduring as the flowing wave,
Forming itself to being in becoming.
Bound yourself, o boundless!

PISCES

May loss find itself in what is lost,
May gain lose itself in gain,
May comprehension seek itself in what is comprehended
And maintain itself in what is maintained,
Raised up to being through becoming,
Interwoven through being to becoming,
May loss be gain for itself!

The virtues

According to a statement that Rudolf Steiner made in a private conversation, the association between the virtues and the twelve constellations of the Zodiac came from Madame Blavatsky, who connected them as follows:

April	Aries	*Devotion*
May	Taurus	*Equilibrium*
June	Gemini	*Perseverance*
July	Cancer	*Unselfishness*
August	Leo	*Compassion*
September	Virgo	*Courtesy*
October	Libra	*Contentment*
November	Scorpio	*Patience*
December	Sagittarius	*Control of Speech*
January	Capricorn	*Courage*
February	Aquarius	*Discretion*
March	Pisces	*Magnanimity*

Rudolf Steiner confirmed these and added, "When one practices these virtues in a certain way, new powers and capacities will arise." According to Ilona Schubert, he then wrote out the following as monthly meditations:

April	Aries	*Devotion becomes Power of Sacrifice*
Taurus	May	*Equilibrium becomes Progress*
Gemini	June	*Perseverance becomes Trust*
Cancer	July	*Unselfishness (Selflessness) becomes Purification*
Leo	August	*Compassion becomes Freedom*
Virgo	September	*Courtesy becomes Tact of Heart*
Libra	October	*Contentment becomes Detachment*
Scorpio	November	*Patience becomes Insight*
Sagittarius	December	*Control of Speech (Thoughts) becomes Sense of Truth*
Capricorn	January	*Courage becomes Power of Redemption*
Aquarius	February	*Discretion becomes Meditative Power*
Pisces	March	*Magnanimity becomes Love*

Steiner advised beginning the practice of a virtue on the twenty-first of the month before the month in question until the first of the following month. For example, for the month of April, one would practice devotion from March 21 to May 1.

The Calendar of the Soul

From "Cosmic Hermit" to "Hieroglyph of the Course of the Year"

Rudolf Steiner wrote the Calendar of the Soul verses (meditations) in 1912. They allow one to follow the course of the year and in so doing cultivate different soul moods and capacities. Two basic movements are enacted. In the summer half of the year (from Easter to Michaelmas, verse 1 to verse 26), the soul lives into the power of the senses so as to be able to receive the cosmic word. During the winter months (from Michaelmas to Palm Sunday, verse 27 to verse 52), the cosmic word itself appears in the soul through the growing power of active, living thinking. Thereby, by our own insight, we are enabled to rise from the prison of our narrow view to become truly cosmic beings. In nature herself, these two movements are articulated by the Earth's exhalation in the light of summer and her inhalation during winter's darkness. The structure is simple. One verse in each group corresponds to a verse in the other: 1 to 52; 2 to 51 ... 26 to 27. Easter to Michaelmas thus creates a kind of first axis. A second axis, however, is created between St. John's Tide and Christmas. Thus there are four related groups of thirteen verses each: two complementing two in a square.

The year, for Steiner, begins with Easter. He even proposed reframing the way we count the years from the first Easter, 33–34 c.e., rather than from Jesus' birth. Therefore the *Calendar 1912/1913*, in which the Calendar of the Soul verses first appeared, was entitled "In the Year 1879 after the Birth of the 'I.'" In his introduction, he explains:

The number of a year is established by each part of humanity so that enumeration begins from an event experienced as especially significant for that part of humanity. The Jews, for instance, calculate the years from what they call "the creation of the world"; Christians, from "the birth of Jesus." In this calendar, however, the years are numbered from the years 33–34 according to the reckoning of the Christian calendar. Thereby, a date in earthly evolution is established that is meaningful for all humanity without distinction of race, nation, and so forth. Thereby, too, is established the acceptance of "spiritual science," which sees in this year the moment when the powers entered human evolution through which—in order to understand itself and think itself into the world—the human "I" was enabled to understand itself in itself and without symbolism through the power of its own thinking life. Before this moment in order to understand themselves and think themselves into the world human beings needed representations and ideas that were taken from the outer world.

The preparation for this moment lies both in ancient Hebrew culture, which first brought to cognition the imageless "God within," and in ancient Greek spiritual life, whose artists and sages also prepared for this moment. They did so insofar as they understood themselves as earthly beings through conceptual thinking, and in their philosophy understood cosmic becoming not through outer images but characterized through concepts that arose only from human "inwardness" as thinking consciousness (Thales to Aristotle). Christian faith expressed the sense of this human fact when it spoke of "the death and resurrection of Christ," or "The Mystery of Golgotha."

Based on all this, the first year from which we calculate the years is the memorial day of this moment. Of course, it may be argued hat counting from the first of January is equally justified. Here, however, it will not happen.

Owen Barfield, when asked what he had gained from a lifetime's study of Anthroposophy, answered, "Some understanding of the living year." In his introduction to the first edition of the *Calendar*, Rudolf Steiner wrote:

As human beings, we feel united with the world and its temporal changes. We find the likeness of the world's archetypal image in our own being. This likeness is no sensory or pedantic imitation of the archetype. What the great world reveals in its temporal flow corresponds to a pendulum swing in our being that does not move in the element of time. Our sensory and perceptual being, we feel, corresponds much more to the nature of summer, woven through with light and warmth. During winter's existence, we sense our-selves much more grounded in ourselves and living in our own thought and will worlds. Thus, the rhythm of inner and outer becomes for us what nature in its temporal alternation presents as summer and winter. A great mystery of existence can rise if we bring our timeless rhythms of perception and thought into corre-spondence with nature's temporal rhythms. If we do so, the year becomes the archetype of human soul activity and thus becomes a fruitful source of true self-knowledge.

In the following annual "soul calendar," we place the human spirit in the changing moods of the year from week to week. Here we can feel our own soul's weaving in the image of the impression of the course of the year. The aim is a "feeling self-knowledge." This feeling self-knowledge can be experienced through these typi-cal weekly verses expressive of soul-life's circular course as timeless in relation to time. However, let it be clearly stated: Our intention is to create the possibility of a path of self knowledge. "Rules" are not given on the model of Theosophical pedants. Rather, indica-tions are given for what could be living weaving of the soul. What-ever is appropriate for souls always takes on an individual coloring. Precisely for this reason each soul must find its way in relation to its own individually honed path. It would be easy to say that if it wishes to cultivate a bit of self knowledge, the soul should medi-tate exactly as it is laid down here. But this is not said, because each person's own path should get its directions on its own, and not just pedantically follow "a path of knowledge."

Spring

Raphael

1. FIRST WEEK — EASTER *[April 7–13]*

> When the Sun speaks to human sense
> from the worlds' vast spaces,
> and from depths of soul
> joy unites with light in seeing,
> then, from sheaths of selfhood,
> thoughts move out to the ends of space
> darkly binding
> human essence to spirit's being.

2. SECOND WEEK AFTER EASTER *[April 14–20]*

> In the outwardness of the senses' universe
> power of thought loses its being,
> and spiritual worlds rediscover
> their new human shoots
> whose seed lies above,
> but whose fruitfulness of soul
> they must find in themselves.

3. THIRD WEEK AFTER EASTER *[April 21–27]*

> The growing human "I,"
> forgetting itself
> and remembering its origin,
> speaks to the universe:
> "In you, I free myself
> from the fetters of idiosyncrasy
> to plumb my true essence."

4. FOURTH WEEK AFTER EASTER *[April 28–May 4]*

"I sense the essence of my essence,"
so speaks feeling,
joining in the Sun-illumined world
with floods of light;
feeling wants to give thinking
warmth for clarity
and closely join in oneness
human beings and the world.

5. FIFTH WEEK AFTER EASTER *[May 5–11]*

In the light that from the depths of spirit
weaves fruitfully in space
and reveals the gods' creating,
the soul's essence appears
expanded to cosmic being
and resurrected
from narrow selfhood's inner power.

6. SIXTH WEEK AFTER EASTER *[May 12-18]*

Out of idiosyncrasy, my self
arises and finds itself
to be the revelation of all worlds
in forces of space and time;
everywhere, the world presents
the truth of my own image
as the archetype of the gods.

7. SEVENTH WEEK AFTER EASTER *[May 19–25]*

My self threatens to escape,
powerfully attracted by the world's light.
Come now prescient, intuitive feeling,
sturdily assume your rights,
replace for me the power of thought
that tends to lose itself
in the senses' blaze of seeming,

8. EIGHTH WEEK AFTER EASTER *[May 26–June 1]*

The senses' might grows
in union with the gods' creating,
depressing my force of thinking
to the dullness of a dream.
Should the divine essence
wish to unite with my soul,
then human thinking quietly
must content itself with dream-being.

9. NINTH WEEK AFTER EASTER *[June 2–8]*

I forget my own will's separateness
and the world's warmth, heralding summer,
fills my soul and spiritual essence;
spirit vision then commands me:
"Lose yourself in light."
Powerfully prescience announces:
"Lose yourself to find yourself."

10. TENTH WEEK AFTER EASTER *[June 9–15]*

The Sun's shining essence
lifts itself to summer's heights
and takes my human feeling with it
into its wide expanses.
Inwardly, sensation stirs with anticipation,
subtly announcing:
"One day you will know
a divine being felt you now."

11. ELEVENTH WEEK AFTER EASTER *[June 16–23]*

In the hour of the Sun, it is up to you
to understand these tidings filled with wisdom.
Surrendered to the beauty of the world,
inwardly feel yourself experiencing:
The human "I" can lose itself
and find itself in the "I" of the world.

12. TWELFTH WEEK AFTER EASTER *[June 24–29]*

ST. JOHN'S TIDE [JUNE 24] VERSE

The brilliance of the world's beauty
forces me from deep within my soul
to lose my own life's godly powers
and soar into the cosmos
to leave myself,
and trustingly seek myself
in cosmic light and warmth.

13. THIRTEENTH WEEK AFTER EASTER *[June 30–July 6]*

> At the height of sensory experience
> flames deep within my soul
> from spirit's fiery worlds
> the true word of the gods:
> "Seek presciently in spirit's grounds
> to find yourself to Spirit related."

Summer

Uriel

14. FOURTEENTH WEEK AFTER EASTER *[July 7–13]*

> Surrendered to the senses' revelation,
> I lost my own being's drive.
> My thoughts became a dream.
> Numbing me, they seemed to rob me of my self.
> But cosmic thinking in the senses' glory
> already approaches to awaken me.

15. FIFTEENTH WEEK AFTER EASTER *[July 14–20]*

> I feel as if entranced
> by the cosmic glory of the spirit's weaving.
> It sheathes my separate being,
> muffling my senses,
> and gives me the strength
> that my I in its narrowness
> is powerless to give itself.

16. Sixteenth week after Easter *[July 21–27]*

So that the maturing gifts of the gods,
fruiting in the soul's core,
might bring selfhood's fruits,
prescience sternly bids me:
"Shelter your spiritual gifts within."

17. Seventeenth week after Easter *[July 28–Aug. 3]*

The cosmic word
that I was permitted to lead
through the senses' gates
deep into my soul, speaks thus:
"Fill the depths of your spirit
with my cosmic vastness
to find me here within you."

18. Eighteenth week after Easter *[Aug. 4–10]*

Can I stretch my soul
so that it unites itself
with the cosmic seed-word it received?
I sense I must find the strength
to form my soul worthily
to become a garment of the spirit.

19. Nineteenth week after Easter *[Aug. 11–17]*

To surround mysteriously
with memory what I have newly received
must be my striving's deeper meaning.
This will awaken
my own strengthening powers within me
which, ever becoming, will give me to myself.

20. TWENTIETH WEEK AFTER EASTER *[Aug. 18–24]*

> For the first time I feel my being,
> which, far from world existence,
> would soon be extinguished in itself
> and building only on its own foundation,
> in itself, would kill itself.

21. TWENTY-FIRST WEEK AFTER EASTER *[Aug. 25–31]*

> I feel a foreign, fruiting force,
> gaining strength to give me to myself,
> I sense the seed germinate
> and prescience weaving within me,
> light-filled, on my selfhood's power.

22. TWENTY-SECOND WEEK AFTER EASTER *[Sept. 1–7]*

> The light that from cosmic widths of space
> lives on powerfully within
> becomes the soul's light
> and shines into the spirit depths
> to release the fruits
> that will in time allow the human self
> to ripen from the world's self.

23. TWENTY-THIRD WEEK AFTER EASTER *[Sept. 8–14]*

> With autumn's coming, the senses' desire
> for stimulation dims.
> The mist's thick veils
> mingle with the light's revelation.
> I myself see in the vast expanses
> autumn's winter sleep.
> Summer has
> surrendered itself to me.

24. TWENTY-FOURTH WEEK AFTER EASTER *[Sept. 15–21]*

Continuously creating itself,
soul being becomes self-aware.
The world spirit strives on,
newly revived in self-knowledge,
and creates from soul darkness
self-consciousness's fruit of will.

25. TWENTY-FIFTH WEEK AFTER EASTER *[Sept. 22–28]*

Now I can belong to myself
and, shining, spread inner light
into the darkness of space and time.
Natural being presses on to sleep.
Soul depths must now awaken
and, waking, bear the Sun's glowing
into cold winter's flowing.

26. TWENTY-SIXTH WEEK *[Sept. 29–Oct. 5]*

MICHAELMAS *[Sept. 29]* VERSE

Nature, I bear your motherly being
in the essence of my will,
whose fiery force
steels my spirit's desires
so that they give birth to self-awareness
to bear myself in me.

Autumn

Michael

27. TWENTY-SEVENTH WEEK AFTER EASTER *[Oct. 6–12]*

Penetrating to the depths of my being,
a yearning filled with prescience
incites me, beholding myself, to find myself
as the gift of the summer Sun that,
like a seed, heating up in this autumn mood,
lives as my soul's powerful impulse.

28. TWENTY-EIGHTH WEEK AFTER EASTER *[Oct. 13–19]*

Inwardly revived again, I can feel
my own being's vastness.
I can pour forth powerful beams of thought
rising from the soul's Sun-like might —
to solve life's mysteries
and give fulfillment to many wishes
whose wings loss of hope had lamed.

29. TWENTY-NINTH WEEK AFTER EASTER *[Oct. 20–26]*

To kindle within me, forcefully, and on my own
the light of thinking,
interpreting the meaning of experience
out of the world spirit's well of power
is now for me summer's legacy,
autumn's peace, and winter's hope.

30. THIRTIETH WEEK AFTER EASTER [Oct. 27–Nov. 2]

The ripe fruits of thinking
now burgeon in the Sunlight of my soul.
My feelings change
to certainty of self-awareness.
Joyfully I sense
autumn's spiritual awakening:
winter will awake
summer in my soul.

31. THIRTY-FIRST WEEK AFTER EASTER [Nov. 3–9]

Light from depths of spirit,
strives outward like the Sun
and becomes life's strong will.
It shines into the senses' dullness
and releases forces
that allow the soul's instinctual
creative powers to ripen in human deeds.

32. THIRTY-SECOND WEEK AFTER EASTER [Nov. 10–16]

I feel my own force bearing fruit,
growing strong to give me to the world;
I feel my own being gaining power,
turning to clarity
in the weaving of life's destiny.

33. THIRTY-THIRD WEEK AFTER EASTER *[Nov. 17–23]*

Now at last I feel that the world,
without my soul's experience of it,
would by itself be frigid, empty life.
Without my experience of it,
it reveals itself as powerless
to create itself anew in souls
and in itself would find only death.

34. THIRTY-FOURTH WEEK AFTER EASTER *[Nov. 24–30]*

Mysteriously, I feel what I have long preserved
revive itself within me
with newly arisen selfhood.
Awakening, it will pour cosmic forces
into my life's outer work.
Growing, it will stamp me into existence.

35. THIRTY-FIFTH WEEK AFTER EASTER *[Dec. 1–7]*

Can I cognize being
so that it finds itself again
in the soul's urge to create?
I feel that power is lent to me
to integrate my own self
modestly into the world self.

36. THIRTY-SIXTH WEEK AFTER EASTER *[Dec. 8–14]*

In my being's depths, the cosmic word,
seeking to be revealed
mysteriously speaks thus:
"To sacrifice yourself through me,
imbue the aims of your work
with my spirit light."

Winter

gabriel

37. THIRTY-SEVENTH WEEK AFTER EASTER *[Dec. 15–21]*

My heart's desire strives blissfully
to bear the light of the spirit
into the world's wintry night.
Then seeds of soul may brightly root
in the world's foundation
and God's word resound in the senses' darkness,
illuminating all being.

38. THIRTY-EIGHTH WEEK AFTER EASTER *[Dec. 22–28]*

CHRISTMAS [DEC. 25] VERSE

As if freed from enchantment, I feel
the spirit child in the soul's womb—
in the brightness of the heart
the holy Word of Worlds has produced
hope's heavenly fruit —
which, from the divine ground of my being,
grows rejoicing into the farthest worlds.

39. THIRTY-NINTH WEEK AFTER EASTER *[Dec. 29–Jan. 4]*

Surrendered to the spirit's revelation,
I gain world being's light.
Power of thinking grows.
Becoming clearer, it gives me to myself,
and, awakening, releases my sense of self
from the thinker's might.

40. FORTIETH WEEK AFTER EASTER *[Jan. 5–11]*

When I am in spirit depths,
in my soul's foundations,
the empty delusion of separateness
fills itself from the heart's worlds of love
with the fiery power of the cosmic Word.

41. FORTY-FIRST WEEK AFTER EASTER *[Jan. 12–18]*

The soul's creative might
strives from the heart's depths
to kindle divine powers
to right action in human life
so that it may shape itself
in human love and human works.

42. FORTY-SECOND WEEK AFTER EASTER *[Jan. 19–25]*

In this winter gloom
the soul's strong urge
is to reveal her own power
and guide it into darkness,
thus anticipating through the heart's warmth,
intuitively the senses' revelation.

43. FORTY-THIRD WEEK AFTER EASTER *[Jan. 26–Feb. 1]*

In depths of winter
spirit's true being grows warm,
giving world appearance the power to exist
through the forces of the heart.
Despite the world's cold,
soul fire inwardly grows strong.

44. FORTY-FOURTH WEEK AFTER EASTER *[Feb. 2–8]*

Grasping new sense attractions,
soul clarity,
remembering the birth of spirit,
fills the bewildering burgeoning of world becoming
with my thinking's creative will.

45. FORTY-FIFTH WEEK AFTER EASTER *[Feb. 9–15]*

The power of thought grows more solid
in union with the spirit's birth,
brightening the senses' dull appeal
to full clarity.
If the soul's fullness
would unite with the world's becoming
then what the senses reveal
must receive the light of thinking.

46. FORTY-SIXTH WEEK AFTER EASTER *[Feb. 16–22]*

The world threatens to numb
my soul's inherent powers.
Therefore, memory, step forth
shining from depths of spirit,
strengthen my vision
that only by strength of will
is able to sustain itself.

47. FORTY-SEVENTH WEEK AFTER EASTER   *[Feb. 23–March 1]*

> The joy of becoming arises
> out of the world's womb,
> quickening the senses' brilliance.
> May it find my force of thinking
> fortified by the divine powers
> living powerfully within me.

48. FORTY-EIGHTH WEEK AFTER EASTER   *[March 2–8]*

> Let the certainty of cosmic thinking now appear
> in the light from cosmic heights
> that streams down powerfully to the soul
> solving the riddles of the soul,
> gathering in the power of its beams,
> awakening love in human hearts.

49. FORTY-NINTH WEEK AFTER EASTER *[March 9–15]*

> "I feel the strength of cosmic being,"
> so speaks clarity of thought,
> recalling its own spirit's growth
> in the dark nights of the world
> and bending its inward rays of hope
> toward the dawning cosmic day.

50. FIFTIETH WEEK AFTER EASTER *[March 16–22]*

Powerfully revealing itself,
and setting loose the forces of its being,
world existence's joy of becoming
speaks to the human "I":
"Into you I bear my life
out of its magic enchantment
and thus attain my true goal."

51. FIFTY-FIRST WEEK AFTER EASTER *[March 23–29]*

The senses' riches pour
into my inner being.
The world spirit finds itself
mirrored in the human eye,
which out of this spirit
must ever create its strength anew.

52. FIFTY-SECOND WEEK *[March 30]*

When from depths of soul
spirit turns to world being,
and beauty streams forth
from the vastness of space,
then, from heavenly distances,
power of life enters our bodies,
uniting, with powerful effect,
spirit's essence with our being.

Meditations for the festivals

Christmas

I

Through the course of the year
summer's power of growth
is exchanged
for winter's earthly peace.
In the course of human life
the power of waking is exchanged
for sleep's peaceful presence.
In both sleeping and waking,
the spirit-filled soul lives on.
Thus, the Earth's soul lives on spiritually
through the exchange of summer and winter.

—From a notebook

II

Christmas Eve (Initiation Night), 1920

The Earth's soul sleeps
in summer's time of heat.
The Sun's image
streams brightly
in external space.

The Earth's soul wakes
in winter's time of cold.
The true Sun
shines spiritually
In inner being.

Summer's joyful day
Is Earth's sleep.
Winter's initiation night
Is Earth's day.

      —For Helene Röschling, Christmas 1920

III

The soul's eye mirrors
The Earth's light of hope

The world's holy wisdom
Speaks to human hearts

The Father's eternal Love
Sends to Earth the Son

Who full of grace gives
Heaven's brightness to humanity's way.

      —Notebook, Christmas 1914

IV

In the depths of the human soul
The Spiritual Sun lives, sure of victory.
The heart's true powers
Can intuit this
In the wintry life within;
The heart's instinct of hope
Beholds the Sun's spiritual victory
In the Christmas light of blessing ·
As the symbol of the highest life
In winter's deep night.

      —Notebook, Christmas Eve 1913

V

Things in space
Speak to the senses,
Changing in time.
The human soul in cognizing—
Unlimited by space,
Untouched by time—
Reaches into the Kingdom of Eternity
—Christmas 1913 (Lecture, December 21, 1913)

VI

Winter Solstice

Behold the Sun
At midnight.
Build with stones
On the lifeless ground.

Find in decline
And in death's night
Creation's new beginning,
Morning's youthful might.

The heights reveal
The Gods' eternal Word.
The depths must guard
The peaceful treasure.

Living in darkness,
Create a Sun.
Weaving in matter
Know spirit's delight.
                    —Lecture, December 17, 1906

VII

The Sunrise of earthly
humanity's becoming—
that is the high secret
on Golgotha's hill.

Daybreak streams forth
In Christmas Light.

In this dawn's
Gentle light
The soul honors
Its own being's
Spirit-related
Power of existence
and source.

—For Helene Röschling, Christmas 1919

VIII

Isis-Sophia
Wisdom of God
Lucifer has slain her,
And on wings of cosmic forces
Carried her away into the depths of space.
Christ-Will
Working in us
Shall tear her from Lucifer
And on grounds of spiritual knowledge
Call to new life in human souls
Isis-Sophia
Wisdom of God.

—December 1920
"The Search for the New Isis, the Divine Sophia"

Meditations from the Esoteric School

The Esoteric School of Theosophy (E.S.) was founded in 1888 by Madame Blavatsky (H.P.B.) and remained under her leadership until her death in 1891. Annie Besant then took over, first with William Q. Judge, then alone after 1895. On October 20, 1902, the German Section of the Theosophical Society was officially founded with Rudolf Steiner as General Secretary and Marie von Sivers (later, Steiner) as Secretary. Annie Besant presided. At this time, Steiner enrolled in the Esoteric School (Marie von Sivers was already a member). Almost immediately, Steiner began functioning as a spiritual teacher, but, as always, teaching only autonomously and out of his own spirit. By July 1904, the Esoteric School under Steiner's leadership was established, and the inner path of Anthroposophy began. The following meditations, aphorisms, and fragments of spiritual teaching deserve and will reward our attention.

I

1. Contemplate: How the point becomes a sphere, yet remains itself. Once you have grasped how the infinite sphere is still a point, return, for then you will see how the infinite can appear in the finite.

2. Contemplate: How the seed corn becomes the ear. Then return, for you will have grasped how what lives, lives in number.

3. Contemplate: How light longs for darkness, heat for cold, man for woman. Then return, for you will have grasped which face the great dragon on the threshold will turn toward you.

4. Contemplate: How you enjoy hospitality in a stranger's house. Then return, for you will have grasped what confronts one who sees the Sun at midnight.

These four sentences are what one calls living sentences. During meditation, they sprout, and shoots of knowledge grow from them.

—From a letter, December 1903

II

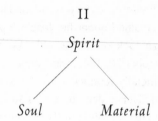

Evolution is the expansion of Spirit outside the Material.

Involution is the contraction of Spirit in the Soul's interior.

No Evolution is possible without corresponding and simultaneous Involution.

No Involution is possible without corresponding and simultaneous Evolution.

III

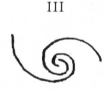

Everything real must be understood as a vortex.

IV

The world is a Vortex.
Every inward spiral must become an outward spiral.
[Life must be a lesson.]
The human being must become a vortex.
Everything performed as a vortex is magic.

V

FATHER
WORD
SPIRIT

The Father reveals himself in the Word
The Word reveals itself to the Spirit
The Spirit reveals itself to the Father

The Father hides in the Son
And reveals himself to the Spirit

The Spirit hides in the Father
And reveals itself to the Son

The Father himself reveals himself.

VI

If you would understand the voice of the spirit from without, you
must first experience your own spirit's being.

If, as a seeker, you no longer desire to hear only the sensory world,
you must search for the one who produced this world. You must live
in thoughts that make the sensory world a world of appearances.

[A version of lines from Blavatsky's *The Voice of the Silence*]
—From a letter, 1904

VII

More radiant than the Sun,
Purer than the Snow,
Subtler than the Ether,
Is the Self,
The Spirit within my heart.
I am that Self,
That Self am I.

—From the Sanskrit (Annie Besant's English version)

VIII

As human beings, we are a stage where the eternal and the transitory meet.

Our knowing is an experience of the eternal, for which we ourselves are the organs of cognition.

Our action is the action of the eternal, for which we ourselves are only mediators.

Understand therefore:

You are the primal spirit's eye—through you, the spirit sees creation.
You are the primal spirit's hand—through you, the spirit creates.

—Notebook, c. 1903

IX

Before the eyes can see, they must be incapable of tears.
Before the ear can hear, it must have lost its sensitiveness.
Before the voice can speak in the presence of the masters,
it must have lost the power to wound.
Before the soul can stand in the presence of the Masters, its feet
must be washed in the blood of the heart.

—From Mabel Collins, *Light on the Path* (E.S. meditation)

X

... After meditation, become absorbed in the following figures, letting them work upon you:

Figure 1:
What is it to disappear
and to rise again out of one's
disappearance?

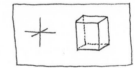

Figure 2:
How does the point become
a circle, and the circle a point?

Figure 3:

What is inside, what is outside?
What is above, what is below?
What is matter, what is spirit?
What is substance, what is etheric ?

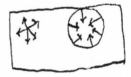

Figure 4:
What is astral ?

Figure 5:
How do the spirits of sensation work on the
bearer of substance?

Figure 6:
How does the turn occur in evolution?
(Involution—Evolution)
Picture this as if the lines were clasps made
of fishbone, but at every moment resisted
their position with all their strength.

—1906 (GA 267)

XI

Light calls the power of germination to life

Spirit calls the power of desire to love

—Notebook, Fall 1904

XII

A U M

A   Past

U   Present—the whole world surrounding us

M   Future—the still unknown for which we live

—1906

XIII

Upper gods
The upper gods work in

Wisdom

from love to wisdom
from wisdom to love

The lower gods
work in love

Lower gods

I bear love in my being's core
I hope with every action

—c. 1907 (GA 267)

XIV

Concentrating on the point between, and somewhat behind, the eyebrows, with the feeling

"Out of the Spirit World my Self flows down to me"

meditate:

I AM

Concentrating on the interior of the larynx, with the feeling

"The Spirit World ensouls the silent Word"

meditate:

It Thinks

Concentrating on the heart, arms, and hands, with the feeling

"The Spirit World creates its own wisdom"

meditate:

She Feels

Then the arms may be folded, or the right hand laid on the left. After a time, one feels how the hands wish to separate by their own power. One should not by any self-deception allow this to occur. Concentrating on the whole bodily surface or the aura (which can be thought of as enclosing the body in an oval sheath), with the feeling

"In me, the Spirit World comes to realization of itself"

meditate:

He Wills

Then, meditation on the solar plexus:

Divine Life

—Composite, 1905–1908

XV

In the pure streams of light
The world's divinity shimmers.
In pure love for all beings
My soul's divine nature rays out.
I rest in the world's divinity;
I will find myself
In the world's divinity.

(*the previous, reversed*):

In the world's divinity
I will find myself.
In it I rest.
The divine nature of my soul rays out
In pure love to all beings.
The world's divinity shimmers
In pure streams of light.

XVI

Meditation Themes, given by Rudolf Steiner:

Know yourself
Firmness
I inhale light, I exhale light
I am persevering
I am spirit
I in me
I understand the essence
I will
Power in my thoughts
Power in me
All above as below/all below as above
Light through me

Light in my thoughts
Light brightness
My stability (perseverance)
My power
My life force
My soul is
Peace in power, power in peace
Peace in strength, strength in peace
Soul in body
Soul harmony
Soul power
Soul light illumines me
Soul warmth penetrates me
Soul warmth streams through me
Soul peace
Blessed peace
Wisdom shines through me
As above, so below

—c. 1906/07

XVII

I rest in the world's divinity.
I live in the world's soul.
I think in the world's spirit.

—Notebook, c. 1906

XVIII

Learn silence and you will have power.
Renounce power and you will have will.
Renounce will and you will have feeling.
Renounce feeling and you will have knowledge.

—1906

XIX

Meditation for Protection from Without:

The (blue) outer sheath of my aura thickens.
It surrounds me with an impenetrable vessel (skin)
Against all impure, unpurified thoughts and sensations.
Only divine wisdom enters it.

—1909

XX

In the mineral realm, the gods sleep;
In the plant realm, the gods dream;
In the animal realm, the gods wake and think.

—c. 1910

XXI

All ways into the spiritual world go through the heart.

—1910

XXII

Thought thinks in thoughts.

XXIII

Wisdom lives in the light (*thought*).
Wisdom streams in the light (*feeling*).
The wisdom of the world streams in the light (*will*).

—1910

XXIV

Love in soul,
Power in willing
Accompany
And support me.
I trust them.
I offer them up.

—Year's end 1912/13

XXV

Three important mantras:

> It thinks me.
> It weaves me.
> It acts me.

It thinks me, because I don't actually think, rather, it thinks me. Exoterically, these three mantras were expressed in [the mystery drama] *The Soul's Probation* in the words, "In your thinking lies cosmic thinking, In your feeling weave cosmic forces, In your willing act cosmic beings." Esoterically, this is expressed by *Ex deo nascimur, In Christo morimur, per spiritum sanctum reviviscimus.*

It thinks me must be permeated *with a feeling of piety.*

It weaves me expresses humanity, what it actually is, and what one is oneself. Self-knowledge should arouse it. The feeling of being entirely woven into the whole of life and the weaving of the world should give birth to this thought, which should be expressed with *a feeling of gratitude.*

It acts me. The whole cosmos, everything, is to be seen as the goal of humanity. *Reverence, devotion, dedication should be the feeling.* One must learn humility and modesty if one wishes to place side by side what one is in one's incompleteness and what the goal of the gods is with regard to humanity.

Ex deo nascimur, In Christo morimur, per spiritum sanctum reviviscimus is the fourth in this series.

—January, 1913

XXVI

The Divine is revealed through Symbols.
The Human is conveyed through Touch.
The Subhuman is averted through the Word.

XXVII

THE FOUR SAYINGS OF THE PILLARS OF WISDOM

This refers to the two giant bronze pillars cast by Hiram of Tyre for Solomon's Temple. The southern pillar was called Jachim (traditionally translated, "he establishes"), the northern one, Boaz (traditionally, "in him is strength"). Steiner refers to these pillars on several occasions. For example on June 20, 1916 (in *Toward Imagination*):

"We enter Earthly life through Jachim, assured that what is there outside in the macrocosm now lives in us, that we are a microcosm, for Jachim means, "the divine poured out over the world is in you."

The other pillar, Boaz, is the entrance into the spiritual world through death. It means roughly this:

"What I have hitherto sought within myself, namely strength, I shall find poured out over the whole world; in it I shall live."

J(achim)   You will find in pure thoughts
           The self that can maintain itself.

           Transmute the thoughts into images
           And you will experience creative wisdom.

B(oaz)   If you thicken feeling into light
           You will reveal the forming power.

           Put your will at the service of beings
           And you will create in world being.

XXVIII

At a certain point, Rudolf Steiner closed the Esoteric Lessons with this meditation:

The germ of my body lay in the spirit.
And the spirit incorporated into my body

Sensory eyes
That I might see through them
The light of bodies.
And the spirit stamped my body
With sensation and thought
And feeling and will
So that through them I might perceive bodies
And work on them.
The germ of my body lay in the spirit.

The germ of the spirit lay in my body
And I will incorporate in my spirit
Suprasensory eyes,
So that I might see the light of spirits.
And I will stamp my spirit
With wisdom and power and love
So that the spirits may work through me
And I become the self-conscious instruments
Of their deeds.
The germ of the spirit lies in my body.

XXIX

PRAYER

O, Powers in the spiritual world,
Let me be outside my physical body,
Let me be knowing in the world of light,
So that I may observe my own light body.
And let the power of the Ahrimanic forces
Be not too strong over me.
Let them not make it impossible for me
To behold what passes in my light body.

—Dornach, January 2, 1916

XXX

I.

The Earth's surface supports me,
The Earth's air envelops me;
Around me I see mountain rocks,
Around me the Earth's plant mantle blossoms.
Sensibility lives in the animal realm
Which divides the fullness of my own being
As though into a thousand single beings.
I feel the strength to rise to ever-new heights.
Only I, a human being, can make such an effort.

2.

I, a human being, was born out of the ground of the Earth.
I was enlivened by Earth's atmosphere,
I am related to the mountain's rocks,
My existence is woven from the plant's mantle,
The animal kingdom supports my spirit's power.
Yet how Earth and rocks and life
Are combined in me into a miracle of harmony!
The Earth's ground will fall away beneath my feet,
Air will become the bearer of death,
The rocks of the mountains will topple down,
The garment of plants will wither away,
The life of animals will be dazed.
But I shall bear the fruits of Earth existence
To a new world-creation of the distant future.
To feel the immortal worth of this goal
Wisdom creates in all thinking,
Beauty conceives in every life breath,
Courage ripens in every pulse beat.

—Esoteric Section

XXXI

Introducing the following mantras, Rudolf Steiner said:

Humanity as a whole is different from individual human beings. Humankind belongs to the organism of the Earth. It creates karma with it. Individuals have their own individual karma. The two should be distinguished properly. In our time, humanity as such is experiencing the meeting with the Guardian of the Threshold. The crossing of the threshold has already begun. It began in the last few years. It is also the beginning of a split in humanity. This is precisely the critical moment that we are confronted by today. The forces that earlier streamed into human beings from the spiritual world are now used up. We are left to ourselves and must now bring these forces up from our unconscious. If humanity does not apply these inner forces, but turns them away, the Mystery of Golgotha will have occurred in vain. This would draw the whole destruction of Earthly evolution in its wake. Souls would still incarnate in bodies, but they would leave these bodies after thirty-three years if they had not taken the spiritual in earlier years into their bodies. Thirty-three-year-olds who had taken up the stream would have to instruct those younger, so that they would be in a position to understand the Mystery of Golgotha....

I will now provide you with some provisions for your way. They can be a great help to you as you meditate. They can bring many secrets into your consciousness.

If you immerse yourself in these words, you will achieve higher knowledge.

Rudolf Steiner wrote the middle three verses first, then the final two (which he placed on the right), then the first (on the left). He noted that feeling is a reflection of dreaming, and that dreams are reflected in feeling. In will, we are still asleep. Therefore, he stressed that the path is one of thinking—that only in thinking is anything possible, even imagining.

I imagine—
This awakens my "I"
For creation-rich
    world-becoming
Which weaves itself
    etherically
Into the world's
    essence.

I think—
This bears my "I"
Into far-distant world
    times
Which preserve
    themselves
In images through "me."

I feel—
This supports my "I"
In the present moment
Which in its being
Weaves as I-experience.

I dream—
This leads my "I"
Through temporal
    events of the present
Which weaves
    etherically
As world action.

I sleep—
This works on me
In world-weaving
    pregnant of the
    future
Which hides
From sensory being.

I will—
This acts in me
In far-distant
    future times
Which form themselves
As seeds through me.

— Esoteric Lesson, February 9, 1920

XXXII

Awaken in thinking: you exist in the spirit light of the world—
Experience yourself as shining/reaching out toward what is shining.

Awaken in feeling: you exist within the spirit deeds of the world.
Experience yourself feeling the spirit deeds.

Awaken in your will: you exist in the spirit being of the world.
Experience yourself in thinking the spirit beings.

Awaken in your "I": you are within your own spirit being.
Experience receiving yourself from the gods/bestowing on yourself.

— Esoteric Lesson, 1920

XXXIII

Divine Sculptor of the Universe
May you feel the smoke of sacrificing souls
Which we let stream reverently
Into your heights of light.

Divine Thinker of the Universe
Take up in your thinking the sacrificial Word
Which we entrust to the circles of air
That meet you when your forces
Lead worlds through space.

Divine Creator of the Universe
Take our being into your Being
So that we may prosper under your protection
When you raise from the Earth depths
A world growing toward the heights of light.

—Esoteric Lesson, May 27, 1923

XXXIV

The stones are mute. I have placed and hidden the eternal Creator-Word in them. Chaste and modest they hold it in the depths.

Materia Prima. Matter hardens itself.

The plants live and grow. I have placed the eternal Creator-Word [of the Sun's power] in them. Sprouting and thriving they carry it into the depths.

Materia Second. Matter opens to the spirit.

The animals feel and will. I have placed [livingly shaped] the eternal Creator-Word in them. Shaping and molding, they hold it in the depths.

Materia Tertia. Matter shines in the soul's light.

Human beings think and act. I have placed the eternal Creator-Word in them [have let it suffer and rejoice in them]. They should feel it from the depths [carry it to the heights].

Spiritus Tertius. The "I" finds itself in the world.

The soul knows and is devoted. I shall release my eternal Creator-Word from her that she may carry it into the heights of purity and piety.

Spiritus secundus. The "I" sacrifices itself to God.

Releasing itself, the soul loves the universe. I speak it in my eternal Creator-Word, awakening and liberating the world in purity. Spiritus primus. The "I" works in God.

—Cognitive Cultic Section

XXXV

THE THREE-PART MANTRA

Rudolf Steiner opened all the esoteric lessons held after World War I with at least the first of these three mantras. The three were used less often together. At least twice, in London, April 16, 1922, and Vienna, September 30, 1923, the last mantra was interwoven with the Rosicrucian sayings *Ex deo nascimur, in Christo morimur, Per spiritum sanctum reviviscimus.*

I

O human being, know yourself
So resounds the cosmic Word
You hear it soul-forcefully
You feel it spirit-mightily

Who speaks so cosmic-powerfully?
Who speaks so heart-inwardly?

Does it work through space's expansive radiance
Into your senses' experience of being?
Does it resound through time's weaving waves
Into your life's stream of becoming?

You yourself are the one who,
In the feeling of space, the experience of time,
Creates the Word, feeling yourself
Estranged in space's soul-emptiness
Because you lose thinking's force
In time's annihilating stream.

2

Cognize first the earnest guardian
Who stands before the door of spirit land
Refusing entrance to your senses' power
And your understanding's might
Because in your senses' weaving
And your thoughts' forming
From space's beinglessness
And time's powers of illusion
The truth of your own being
Must raise you first.

3

I step into this sensory world
Bringing with me thinking's harvest
A god's power has brought me in
[EDN. *Ex deo nascimur. From God we are born.*]
Death stands at the path's end—
I will feel the being of Christ—
It awakens in matter's dying spirit birth.
[I. Ch. M *In Christo morimur. In Christ we die.*]
In spirit I find the world
And know myself in world becoming.
[P.S.S.R. *Per spiritum sanctum reviviscimus.*
Through the Holy Spirit we live again.]

XXXVI

If the gods had only
Consumed themselves in joy
The world would never have existed
They would only have scattered their own being
In the atmosphere of the Earth
Sad they would have become
And lamenting
Embraced their own being
And out of their lamentation
Arose the holy FIAT
The world-creating Word.

Joy is the fire
That shines forth
When lamentation
Melts into ashes.

XXXVII

J A O U E (A sound meditation)

J   Stillness within you

A   You open to the world, which speaks

O   The angles come—join hands

U   The second hierarchy follows, surround you with light

E   The first hierarchy comes, burning you with fire

—Esoteric Lesson, May 27, 1923

XXXVIII

In a written note to the following beautiful meditation, Edith Maryon notes, "butterfly = thought."

Butterfly Meditation

Catch the butterfly.
Send it to the icy heights
Where world-dreams reign.
If it becomes a bird for you
Then you have done
Half the work.
Plunge the bird
Into the ocean depths
Where the world-will works.
Now it still remains for you
To purify in fire, to burn
The bird's corpse.
Then consume the ash,
And you are
Light in world darkness.

XXXVIX

Truth, Wisdom, Immeasurability, O God,
Blessedness, Eternity, Beauty,
Peace, Blessing, Non-Duality
On me (AUM)
Peace, Peace, Peace.

Satyam jnanam anantam brahma
Ananda rupam amritam bibharti
Shantam shivam advaitam
On, shatih, shatih, shantih.

—1923

The Rosicrucian Path

Whoever overcomes themselves will be free of the power that binds all beings.

— Rosicrucian Saying,
Esoteric lesson, March 3, 1906

Rudolf Steiner spoke of three ways: what he called the way of "yoga": the Christian" or "Christian-Gnostic" way; and the "Rosicrucian" way. The three ways are not mutually exclusive but overlap in many ways. They may be said to be distinguishable, but not necessarily divisible. In Steiner's description, the three differ most radically with regard to their relationship to a teacher or guru. Everything follows from that. The yoga path depends upon complete surrender to a living, embodied teacher; while in the Christian way, the path of Christ, there is no individual guru, only Christ himself, the Master and Teacher. However, as Steiner emphasizes, it is often an earthly teacher who leads the student to Christ. The Rosicrucian path, for its part, gives the student the greatest independence. The earthly teacher becomes an adviser or spiritual friend. There is collegiality, and the sense of "an invisible college," in which students and teacher are united. There is a further difference in the three ways. We may call it a difference of emphasis or method. The yoga way (as interpreted by Steiner) begins with the embodied being and uses the breath and different parts and organs of the body (legs, arms, hands, feet, lungs, heart, liver, etc.) in meditation. The Christian path works more with the interaction of soul and spirit in prayer and daily life, and tries to hold to love as its beginning and end. "Thinking" (in the sense of "living thinking") lies at the heart of Rosicrucian practice. Steiner himself practiced and taught all three ways.

The path

The Rosicrucian path leaves the student with the greatest possible independence. The guru in this case is no longer a leader but an adviser who gives directions for the necessary inner training. At the same time, the guru assures that, along with esoteric training, there is a specific development of thinking, without which no esoteric training can be accomplished. This is because there is something about thinking that does not apply to anything else.

While on the physical plane, we perceive what is there only with the physical senses. Astral perceptions are valid for the astral plane; devachanic hearing is valid only in devachan. Thus, each plane has its own specific form of perception. But one activity—logical thinking—goes through all worlds. Logic is the same on all three planes. Thus, on the physical plane you can learn something that is valid also for the higher planes. This is the method followed by Rosicrucian training when, on the physical plane, it focuses primarily on thinking, and for this purpose uses the means available on the physical plane. Penetrative thinking can be cultivated by studying spiritual scientific truths, or by practicing thought exercises. Anyone who wishes further training for the intellect can study books such as *Truth and Science* and *Intuitive Thinking as a Spiritual Path: A Philosophy of Freedom*. These books were written as a deliberate training for thinking, to enable thinking to move with certainty on the highest planes. Even those who study these books and know nothing of spiritual science can find their way in the higher worlds. But, as I have said, spiritual scientific teachings act in the same way as the system of Rosicrucian training: The truest inner guide is one's own clear thinking. Thus, a guru will be simply a friend and adviser, because training one's thinking also trains the best guru for oneself. Of course, you still need a guru to provide advice on how to advance independently toward freedom.

Among Europeans, the Christian way is best for those whose *feelings* are most strongly developed. On the other hand, there are those who have broken away somewhat from the Church and rely more on science. Science, however, has led them into a doubting attitude of mind. Such people will do best with the Rosicrucian way.

—Lectures, September 2–5, 1906

Primary training

Preliminary Rosicrucian training involves seven stages, which need not be accomplished in the sequence enumerated here....

I.   Study [thinking]
2.   Acquisition of Imaginative knowledge
     ["All transitory phenomena are simply symbols."]
3.   Acquisition of the esoteric script
4.   Bringing rhythm into life
     [also described as "preparing the philosopher's stone"]
5.   Knowledge of the microcosm, our essential human nature
6.   Union with the macrocosm, or great universe
7.   Attaining beatitude

—Lecture, March 14, 1907

Rosicrucian study

We study, in the Rosicrucian sense, when we have thoughts that no longer have any relationship to the sensory world. The West is familiar with sense-free thinking only in geometry. Gnostic-Christian schools gave the name *mathesis* to thoughts related to higher truths, to God, and to the higher worlds, because insights such as mathematical understanding must be acquired without the senses. A circle drawn with chalk is far from perfect; a true circle is possible only in thought....

Good ways of learning pure thinking can be found in my books *Truth and Science* and *Intuitive Thinking as a Spiritual Path*. These books exercise sense-free thinking.

—Lecture, June 28, 1907

The Rose Cross

The mystic center of Rosicrucianism is the symbol of the Rose Cross: the black cross with seven roses. One of the primary practices taught by Steiner is the meditation (and visualization) of this image. We begin with the classic description of meditating the Rose Cross from *An Outline of Esoteric Science*.

We can rise to a state of suprasensory consciousness only from ordinary waking consciousness, the condition in which the soul lives prior to its ascent. Training provides the soul with means that lead it out of the ordinary waking state. Among the first methods provided by the training discussed here are some that can still be described as functions of ordinary waking consciousness.

The most important of these methods involves silent activities of the soul. The soul devotes itself to certain specific mental images that contain the power to awaken certain hidden faculties in the soul. Such mental images are not like those of ordinary daily life, whose purpose is to depict external phenomena; and the more truly they accomplish this, the "truer" such images are. In this sense, it is part of their essential nature to be "true." This, however, is not the goal of the mental images the soul concentrates on when its purpose is spiritual training. Images intended for spiritual training are structured so that they do not reproduce anything external, but have an awakening effect on the soul.

The best mental, or thought, pictures for this purpose are symbolic, though others can also be used. The substance of such mental images is unimportant; the point is for the soul to devote all its energy to emptying its consciousness of everything except the given mental image.

In our everyday soul life, the soul's energies are divided among many different things, and our mental images shift rapidly. In spiritual training, the point is to concentrate the soul's whole activity on a single mental image, freely chosen as a focus of awareness. Consequently, symbolic images are better than those that represent outer objects or processes and are connected with the external world, since they do not force the soul to rely on itself, as do the symbols created through its own energy. The object of imagination is unimportant. What is important is that the process of visualizing the image frees the soul from dependence on anything physical.

By recalling what happens in memory, we can begin to understand what it means to immerse ourselves in a visualized image.

For example, if we look at a tree and then turn away from it so that we can no longer see it, we can reawaken the mental image of the tree out of our memory. The mental image we have of a tree when it is not actually present before our eyes is the memory of the tree.

Let us imagine that we retain this memory in our soul. We allow the soul to rest on this memory image and attempt to exclude all other images until the soul is immersed in the memory image of the tree. In this case, however, although the soul is immersed in a mental image, the image is a copy of something perceived through the senses. But if we attempt the same thing with an image we insert into our consciousness through a free act of volition, we are gradually able to achieve the necessary effect. I will illustrate this with a single example of contemplating, or meditating, on a symbolic mental image.

First, this mental image must be built up in the soul. I can do this as follows: I imagine a plant taking root in the ground, sprouting one leaf after another, and continuing to develop up to the point of flowering. Then I imagine a human being alongside this plant. In my soul, I bring the thought to life that this human being has qualities and abilities that we can call more perfected than those of the plant. I think of how human beings can move freely in response to feelings and intentions, whereas plants are fixed in the ground. But then I also notice that, although human beings are certainly more perfected than plants are, they also have characteristics that we do not perceive in plants—characteristics whose absence can, in fact, make plants seem more perfected than humans are. Human beings are filled with desires and passions, which their actions follow, and certain mistakes result from those drives and passions. In contrast, I see how plants obey the pure laws of growth, developing one leaf after another and opening their flowers without passion to the Sun's innocent rays. I can say that human beings have an advantage over plants in terms of a certain kind of perfection, but that the price paid for this perfection is that urges, desires, and passions have been allowed to enter human nature, in contrast to the forces of the plants that seem so pure to me.

Next, I visualize green sap flowing through the plant. I imagine this as an expression of the pure, passionless laws of growth. Then I visualize red blood flowing through human arteries and imagine it as an expression of urges, desires, and passions. I allow all this to arise in my soul as a vivid thought.

Now I think about how human beings are capable of development, how they can use the higher soul faculties to cleanse and purify their urges and passions. I think about how this destroys a baser element in these urges and passions, which are then reborn on a higher level. The blood may then be imagined as the expression of these cleansed and purified urges and passions. For example, in the spirit I see a rose and say: In the red sap of the rose blossom I see the color of the plant's green sap transformed into red, and the red rose, like the green leaf, obeys the pure, passionless laws of growth. Let the red of the rose symbolize the blood that is an expression of purified urges and passions. They have been stripped of their baser element and are now similar in purity to the forces that are active in the red rose.

At this point, I try not only to assimilate these thoughts with my intellect, but also to bring them to life in my feeling. I can have a blissful sensation when I imagine the growing plant's purity and absence of passion; I can generate a feeling in myself for the price human beings must pay for greater perfection by acquiring urges and desires. This can transform my earlier bliss into a serious feeling. Next, a feeling of liberating happiness can stir in me as I devote myself to the thought of the red blood that can become the vehicle of inwardly pure experiences, just like the red sap of the rose blossom. It is important not to think the thoughts that serve to build up a symbolic mental image unaccompanied by feeling.

After living in these thoughts and feelings for a while, we can transform them into a symbolic image as follows: Imagine a black Cross. Let this be the symbol of the baser element that has been eliminated from our urges and passions. Imagine seven radiant red roses arranged in a circle at the intersection of the two beams of the Cross. Let these symbolize the blood that expresses the cleansed purified passions and urges. This symbolic image must now be evoked for the mind's eye as described in relation to a memory picture. A symbolic mental image like this has the power to awaken our souls when we inwardly immerse ourselves in it with devotion. Try to exclude all other mental images while immersed in this way. As vividly as possible, allow this symbol alone to linger in spirit before the mind's eye.

It is important that this symbol not be proffered immediately as a soul-awakening image, but built up first with specific ideas about plants and human beings, since the effectiveness of this kind of symbol depends on its being assembled in this way before one uses it for meditation. If we imagine it without first going through this buildup in our souls, the symbol remains cold and has much less effect than when it receives soul-illuminating force through such preparation.

During meditation, however, do not summon all of the preparatory thoughts. Allow only the image to linger vividly in the spirit, while permitting the feeling that results from the preparatory thoughts to resonate. In this way, the symbol becomes a token of the feeling experience, and its effectiveness arises from the fact that the soul dwells on that experience. The longer one dwells on it without the intervention and disruption of any other images, the more effective the whole process will be. It is also a good idea to frequently repeat the described process of building the image—outside the time set aside for the actual meditation—through thoughts and feelings, so that the feeling does not fade. The more patience one has in renewing it, the more significant the image becomes for the soul....

The purpose of this Rose Cross symbol is to demonstrate the process of effective meditation. In spiritual training, one can use any number of images of this kind, and they can be built up in many different ways. Certain sentences, phrases, or single words may also be assigned as subjects for meditation. The purpose of all of these methods of meditation, however, is to tear the soul away from sensory perception and rouse it to a kind of activity in which physical sensory impressions have no meaning; the essential thing is to awaken dormant inner soul faculties.

—*An Outline of Esoteric Science*

Meditations

Rosicrucianism is a path of practice. Throughout his life Rudolf Steiner gave many indications and meditation practices to his students that were explicitly Rosicrucian in nature. Here are a few of the meditations he gave.

I

Imagine the Cross arising from burning wood. Then, on the Cross, the seven reddish roses, separate from it, and gradually becoming illuminated:

First Rose, lighting up: the left half of the head

May your warmth warm through me.

Second Rose, lighting up: the right half of the head

May your light shine through me.

Third Rose, lighting up: left hand

May your awakeness stream through me.

Fourth Rose, lighting up: right hand

May your peace pour through me.

Fifth Rose, lighting up: left foot

> *May your ray move powerfully through me.*

Sixth Rose, lighting up: right foot

> *May your raising up penetrate me.*

Seventh Rose, lighting up: above

> *I am in your sphere.*

II

(*evenings*) The image of a bright space, becoming ever darker; a
white Cross with seven green Roses:

In this sign I behold
The Revelation of the all-encompassing Spirit
A part of which is my own being—
Awake, o holy longing,
In my soul's deepest depths
To sense, to feel, to know
My own spirit in cosmic spirit.

(*mornings*) Image of a dark space, which becomes ever brighter; a
black Cross with red Roses:

I strive to enter
My soul's depths
So that out of the darkness
The light of the spirit might arise
And awaken in me
The spirit of this sign
To which I surrender myself.

—E.S., May 1912

III

Pour through me full of power,
flow wakefully streaming,
streaming from below upward,
strengthening above in the spirit,
strengthening through the source of life,
the source of life, that descends,
descends from the being of the Sun
through me.

—For Suse Karstsens

IV

I raise my eyes
To the black wooden Cross
And surrender myself with my soul
Into the power of the World Spirit;
As the black Cross gives itself
Wholly to the light.

V

Bright Rose Stars
On the black wooden Cross
May they be an image for me
Of my soul's divine spiritual powers
Streaming in the dark soul's ground in me.

—c. 1913

VI

On the black Cross
Bright Rose Stars image
In my soul's depths
Of strong shining spiritual powers
Active in me.

—November 9, 1913

VII

Seven bright Rose Stars
On a black wooden Cross
Seven powerful soul forces
In the welter of life: strength, peace, striving for wisdom,
   the power of love, detachment, attention, trust/confidence.
With these signs I inscribe my soul.

—June 1913

VIII

I see seven Rose Stars gleaming
On the black wood of the Cross—
May they make me full of power
So that I may experience and sense
Seven World Powers within me
That work within my human being.

—1915 or later

Signature of the Rose Cross School

Going back to the original documents of the early seventeenth century, the signature of the Rosicrucians has always been: From God we are born; In Christ we die; Through the Holy Spirit we are reborn. This threefold movement epitomizes the inner path that Steiner taught, and he never tired of repeating it and understanding it in different ways. It sums up not only the individual path, but also the very foundation of creation and cosmology.

I

Ex Deo nascimur
In Christo morimur
Per Spiritum Sanctum reviviscimus.

—Munich, May 1907

II

I am born from God
I die in Christ
I resurrect through the Holy Spirit.

—Malsch, April 1909

III

The Rosicrucian formula is exoteric when one says it in full. It is esoteric, when it is said as follows:
Ex Deo nascimur, In ——— *morimur. Per Spiritum Sanctum revisicimus.*
You yourself must find the great difference between these in your own soul.

—c. 1910

IV

The saying, *Ex deo nascimur. In Christo morimur* can in mysticism also be turned: In Christ *we live.*

—Esoteric Lesson, February 12, 1911

V

From God's being, the human soul arises
Dying, the soul can dip down into the essential ground
One day, it will unite death to the spirit.

—Munich, August 1911

VI

From the divine, the human being IS.
In Christ, life becomes death.
In cosmic-spirit-thought, the soul awakens.

—Dornach, January 1924

Rosicrucian meditations

The following are two Rosicrucian Meditations—adapted and freely rendered by Rudolf Steiner—from The Secret Symbols of the Rosicrucians of the sixteenth and seventeenth centuries (Geheime Figuren der Rosenkreutzer aus dem 16ten und 17ten Jahrhundert, Altona 1785).

I. FIRE MEDITATION

Fire (*Ignis Philosophorum invisibilis et secretissimus occultatum*: Philosophical Fire, invisible and most secretly hidden)

Strive for the fire
Seek the fire
The fire will come to you
Kindle the fire
Add onto the fire
Cook fire in fire
Throw body, soul, and spirit into the fire
Then you have dead and living fire
It will become black, yellow, white, red fire
Bear your children into the fire
Feed, give them to drink, and nourish them in the fire
So they live and die in the fire
And are fire and remain in the fire
Their silver and gold all become fire
And finally become a fourfold philosophical fire.

The notes to these meditations refer to the Saturn phase of the Earth's evolution. Earth was then a sphere of warmth, black light, a hidden glimmering fire: a principle of warmth, or fire. We carry the memory in our blood: its warmth (fire). Through evolution we have had "four" kinds of blood: black (no light) blood (or fire) during the Saturn stage of evolution; yellow, light-filled blood (or fire) during the Sun stage; white blood (or fire) during the Moon stage; red blood (or fire) during the Earth stage.

The heat of warmth we have in our blood today is the heat of the planet Saturn.

These different kinds of blood, or fire, remain in us and act as the instruments for spirits that work within and on us, until we become sufficiently individualized to assume all the functions that these spirits have exercised....

The way to the control of our own instrument is shown in the first line.

The four kinds of fire relate to the essence of our four lower sheaths [sensory body, life body, desire body, understanding]; these are "children of the "I'." They must be "burned" in the fire of the spirit so that we may become the fourfold philosophical fire during the Vulcan period. We must "add" fire to fire; the fire of lower passions must be purged through union with the higher, spiritual fire.

II. WATER MEDITATION

Water (*Aqua Philosophorum: Mercurius Primaterialis Catholicus,*
The Water of the Philosophers: mercurial primal catholic.)

Water is water and remains water
From the heaven of the wise water rains
The stone of the wise weeps tear water
Yet the world pays such water no heed,
Its fire burns in the water
And lives in the water

Out of fire make water
And cook fire in water
Then you will have fiery water
Like a sharp salty ocean-water
To your children it is a living water!
But consume body and soul to water—
It becomes stinking, green, rotten, blue like heaven water
Digest, calcinate, dissolve, and putrefy the water;
Seek the philosophers' fourfold permanent water
And when it is best made
Art will become water.

* * *

Two sayings to support oneself in meditation:

Guard yourself in your esoteric striving from being *drowned.*

Guard yourself against *burning* your own "I" in the fire.

* * *

Two ways that lead us into the spiritual world:

The first way is to go out into the macrocosm. The experience that we have there is like being *drowned* in fear. It is particularly powerful for those who are not carefully prepared.

The second way leads down into our own souls. It is the descent into the microcosm. There it is like being *burnt* in shame.

* * *

A MEDITATION

I turn to things,
I turn with my senses.
Sense being, you deceive me!
What flees existence as nothing
Is being and essence to you.
May what must seem to you worth nothing
Reveal itself within me!
Spirit Light, warm me,
Let me feel myself willing in you.
What is well thought, cognized truth,
How luminously I experience you!
Weaving error, badly thought out
Show yourself to the beacon of my soul
That I may be weaving in myself.
Luminous I and beacon-soul,
Soar above true being of becoming
What is thought out, what cognized
Condenses now to spirit being.
And like light pearls of existence
There dwells in the sea of divine truth
What deceives the senses' existence.

The way of Christian Rosenkreutz

Five sentences guide souls who wish to follow Christian Rosenkreutz and work in human life:

1. Think only out of the spirit that reveals itself in the creations of nature. See human works as a continuation of nature's works.

2. Place all work in the service of human impulses, but make those impulses meditate the works of the spirit.

3. Lovingly serve human beings, so that the creative spirit can reveal itself in the relationship between one human being and another.

4. Do not allow any value offered by the world to lead you astray from the value that the spirit confers upon all human labor.

5. Do not, like bad alchemists (or "puffers"), make the mistake of confusing the physical with the spiritual.

— An Essay on *The Chemical Wedding of Christian Rosenkreutz,*" 1917

The Christian-Gnostic Path

Although it may be said that the path of Anthroposophy is simply a path of cognition, a cognitive method, it is nevertheless indisputable that, for Rudolf Steiner, the Christ was the central, indispensable aspect of the path, as it was of the cosmos. Christ as theme and Christ as way is everywhere in his work. Only at the beginning, however, did he lay it out as a separate way. Later, one may say that it became the way itself.

The Christian path

The Christian path replaces individual gurus with one great guru for everyone—the leader of humanity, Jesus Christ. The sense of belonging to Jesus Christ and being united with him can replace surrender to an individual guru. But the student must first be led to Christ by an earthly teacher; in a certain sense, one still depends on a guru on the physical plane....

The Christian way can be followed with the advice of a teacher who knows the requirements and can rectify errors at every step. Keep in mind, however, that in Christian training the great guru is Jesus Christ himself. Hence it is essential to firmly believe in Christ's presence and life on Earth. Without this, a feeling of union with him is impossible. Furthermore, we must recognize that the Gospel of St. John is a document that originates with the great guru and can itself be a source of instruction. Beyond merely believing, we can experience this Gospel within our being. By absorbing it in the right way, you find Jesus Christ and thus no longer need to prove the reality of Jesus Christ.

In Christian training you must meditate on this Gospel, not simply read and reread it. The Gospel begins: "In the beginning was the Word, and the Word was with God, and the Word was God." When understood correctly, these opening verses of the Gospel become sentences for meditation to be absorbed inwardly in the state of *dhyana* [meditation on concepts that have no sensory perceptible counterpart]. In the morning, before other impressions have entered the soul, if you live for five minutes solely in these sentences, with everything else excluded from your thoughts, and if you continue to do this over the years with complete patience and perseverance, you will find that these words are not meant merely to be understood; you will realize that they have spiritual power, and through them you will indeed experience a transformation of the soul. In a certain sense, you become clairvoyant through these words, so that everything in St. John's Gospel can be seen with astral vision.

Then, with the direction of a teacher and after meditating again on the five opening verses, allow the first chapter to pass through your mind for seven days. During the following week, after again meditating on the five opening verses, move on to the second chapter and continue in the same way through the twelfth chapter. You will soon realize the power of this experience; you are taken into the events in Palestine (as inscribed in the akashic record) when Jesus Christ lived there, and you realize that you can in fact experience it all. Once you reach the thirteenth chapter, you must experience the individual stages of Christian initiation.

The first stage is *Washing the Feet*. We must understand the significance of this great scene. Jesus Christ bends before those who are lower than himself. Such humility toward those who are lower than we are, and at whose expense we have been able to rise, must be present everywhere in the world. If a plant were able to think, it would thank the minerals for giving it the ground on which to lead a higher form of life; the animal would have to bow before the plant and say, "I owe to you the possibility of my very existence." Likewise, we should recognize what we owe to the rest of nature. Likewise, in our society, a person in a higher position should bow before those who are lower and say, "Without the diligence of those who labor on my behalf, I would not be in my present position." It is like this through all stages of human existence, up to Jesus Christ himself, who bows in meekness before the apostles and says, "You are my ground, and to you I fulfil the saying, 'One who would be first must be last, and the one who would be Lord must be the servant of all.'" Washing the Feet indicates this willingness to serve—this bowing in perfect humility. Everyone committed to esoteric development must have this feeling.

Those imbued with such humility have experienced the first stage of Christian initiation. Two signs—an inner and an outer—indicate when you have done so. The outer sign is a feeling that your feet are being bathed in water. The inner sign is an astral vision that comes quite specifically: You witness yourself washing the feet of others. This picture arises in dreams as an astral vision, and every student has this same vision. Once you have experienced it, you have truly absorbed this whole chapter.

The second stage is the *Scourging*. When you have reached this point, while reading of the Scourging and allowing it to work on you, you must develop another feeling. You learn to stand firm under the heavy strokes of life, telling yourself, "I will stand up to whatever pains and sorrows come my way." The outer sign is that you feel a kind of prickling pain all over your body. The inner sign is a dream vision of seeing yourself being scourged.

The third stage is the *Crowning with Thorns*. Here, you must acquire yet another feeling: You learn to stand firm, even when you are scorned and ridiculed because of all that you hold most sacred. The outer sign of this is the experience of a severe headache; the inner indication is an astral vision of yourself being crowned with thorns.

The fourth stage is the *Crucifixion*. A new and very specific feeling must now be developed. You no longer consider your body to
be your most important possession; you become just as indifferent
to your body as you would be toward a mere piece of wood. Then
you attain an objective view of the body you carry through life; you
see your body as the "wood of the Cross." There is no need to
despise it, any more than you would any tool. As the outer sign of
reaching this stage, something like red stigmata appear on the body
during meditation, precisely at the places called the "sacred
wounds." They actually appear on the hands and feet and on the
right side of the body at the level of the heart. The inner sign is to
see yourself hanging on the Cross.

The fifth stage is the *Mystical Death*. Now a student experiences
the nothingness of earthly things and, in fact, dies for a while to all
earthly things.

One can give only the slightest descriptions of the later stages of
Christian initiation. A student experiences, in an astral vision,
darkness reigning everywhere; the earthly world has fallen away. A
black veil spreads over what is to come. While in this condition, a
student comes to know all that exists as evil and wickedness in the
world. This is the *Descent into Hell*. You experience the rending of
the curtain, and the devachanic world appears; this is the *Rending of
the Veil* of the Temple.

The sixth stage is that of the *Burial*. At the fourth stage, one
learns to see one's body objectively; now you develop a feeling that
everything around you in the world is just as much part of what
truly belongs to you as your own body is. The body extends far
beyond its skin; you cease to be a separate being and are united
with the whole planet. Earth has become your body; you are buried
in the Earth.

The seventh stage, the *Resurrection*, cannot be described in words.
Esotericism thus teaches that the seventh stage can be conceived only
by one whose soul has been freed entirely from the brain; and it
can be described only to one who has achieved this. Consequently,

I can do no more than mention it here. A Christian teacher indicates the path to this experience.

For one who has lived through this seventh stage, Christianity has become an inner soul experience. Such a person is wholly united with Jesus Christ, who is in that individual.

—September 5, 1906

Christian-Gnostic meditations (1906–1908)

I

1. *Early in the morning*, immediately after awaking, before any impressions have passed through your soul, try to free your consciousness totally of all memories of everyday life, and to turn your attention away from all outer perceptions. Having achieved this inner stillness, allow only one thing to live in your soul: *The first five verses of the Gospel according to John.*

2. For the first fourteen days, this is followed every day by an attempt to place the entirety of your own life before your soul, in order to get to know yourself completely. After these fourteen days, go through the entire Gospel of John, dwelling on one chapter every day for seven days. That is, for the first seven days, chapter 1 from verse 6 through the end, and for the second seven days, chapter 2, and so on.

Having arrived at chapter 13:

The washing of the feet:

Attempt to experience the feeling of how each higher being owes its existence to those below and must therefore bow humbly to them.

The scourging:

Dwell on feeling the ability to stand upright under the blows that life deals you with all its pain and suffering.

The crowning with thorns:

Dwell on the need to stand upright, even when confronted by every kind of derision and mockery.

The Crucifixion:

Dwell on the feeling that the body you carry with you is foreign, and that you are bound to it from outside.

The mystic death:

Experience the curtain still covering the spiritual world. Then experience how it is rent asunder and you see into the spiritual world. In this way, you learn to see the depths of evil: the descent into hell.

The entombment:

Feel united with all earthly beings and with the Earth itself. Immerse yourself in this feeling.

The Resurrection:

It must be experienced; the words of ordinary language are inadequate to describe it.

3. Call to mind the figure of Jesus Christ, then go on to this thought, immersing yourself in it for a long time: *I, in Your Spirit.*

* * *

Evening: Look back over all the day's events.

Parts 1 and 3 are the same every day; only part 2 changes, as described, after every seven days.

After completing the cycle of part 2, begin again from the beginning, again and again.

After a long time, it becomes possible to experience the inner and outer *symptoms* that describe inner Christian development:

Inwardly:	Outwardly:
You feel as though your feet are immersed in water.	You envision performing the washing of the feet yourself.
Something like a burning sensation all over your skin.	You envision yourself being flogged.
You feel pain in your head.	You envision yourself wearing the crown of thorns.
The stigmata redden during meditation.	You envision yourself hanging on the Cross.

II

BREVIARY-LIKE MEDITATION FOR A CATHOLIC PRIEST

It is necessary to meditate *every morning* for *an entire year,* by immersing yourself completely for half an hour in the verses indicated:

Month:	Verse in St. John	Month:	Verse in St. John
First:	I:1–2	Seventh:	I:9
Second:	I:3	Eighth:	I:10
Third:	I:4	Ninth:	I:11
Fourth:	I:5	Tenth:	I:12
Fifth:	I:6	Eleventh:	I:13
Sixth:	I:7–8	Twelfth:	I:14

This is to be followed by another meditation that runs through all the weeks of the year, whereby you fully immerse yourself in the verses indicated for fifteen minutes:

Day 1	(Sunday):	Genesis 1:1–5
Day 2	(Monday):	Genesis 1:6–8
Day 3	(Tuesday):	Genesis 1:9–13
Day 4	(Wednesday):	Genesis 1:14–19
Day 5	(Thursday):	Genesis 1:20–23
Day 6	(Friday):	Genesis 1:24–31
Day 7	(Saturday):	Genesis 2:1–3

It should be understood that the periods of time indicated in these and other exercises are not to be regulated by the clock, but according to the feeling for time that you acquire. The substance of all of the biblical words belonging to this meditation are to be imagined pictorially; they are to be transformed into images as much as possible. For example, John 1–2 would look like this: the image of a great and mighty sphere, and within this sphere, all substance is moving in such a way that it takes shape according to the meaning and significance of the "divine word" resounding through it. My lectures supply building blocks in the sense of the esoteric Christian tradition; they can guide the soul to transform the words of the Bible into the appropriate, authentic images. It is important to stick to these building blocks as much as possible.

After this morning meditation, the following should be added *every day* in profound meditation for *at least* fifteen minutes:

I am trying to understand that, during the first third of cosmic evolution, Christ was the leader of a band of spirits in whose bosom I existed unconsciously, and that to achieve consciousness I had to separate from this band of spirits until Yahweh had prepared my soul to the point of being able to receive the Christ forces consciously. Now I can receive them if I turn my spiritual sight toward the Christ become flesh and accept his being into my being. In this process, you must think of the being of Christ as portrayed in the Gospel of John.

Throughout the day, immerse your soul in the four parts of the Mass:

I. *Gospel:*
Think of it as the way in which the "Word of God" reaches human beings, as far as the intellect is concerned.

2. *Offering:*
Think of it as freely offering to God whatever part of God's being is already within you.

3. *Transubstantiation:*
Imagine the sacrificed human element being truly transformed into the divine.

4. *Communion:*
Imagine yourself united with God.

During the evening, work on acquiring the seven attributes of the Christian mystic, as follows:

I. *The feeling of true humility:*
Everything higher owes its existence to something lower—the plant to the stone, the animal to the plant, higher human beings to the lower. Image: the washing of the feet, Christ bending down to the disciples.

2. *The feeling of patient suffering:*
I will patiently bear all of life's pain and suffering. Image: the scourging.

3. *The feeling of strength and courage:*

I will stand upright, even when what is holiest to me is disparaged. Image: the crowning with thorns.

4. *The feeling of independence from the body:*

I will carry my body as if it were foreign, like the wood of the Cross. Image: carrying the Cross.

5. *The feeling of mystical death:*

I will learn to live in that aspect of myself that is not the body, over which death has no power. Image: hanging on the Cross.

6. *The feeling of being buried and resurrected:*

I consider the whole Earth to be my body.

7. *The feeling of ascending to heaven*

follows naturally from the previous feelings; there are no human words to express it.

This is followed every evening by the review of the day's events in reverse order, so that you begin with your last experience in the evening and conclude with the first one in the morning.

Outward rules to observe: As much as possible, practice abstinence. Each time you resist desire, it leads you to cease a previous desiring, bringing you one step closer to *insight*.

Exercises are to be continued until new ones are given. After awhile, however, [the teacher] should be told what the person wishes to do.

Study is necessary for everything that leads to absorption in cosmic evolution and the nature of the human being.

* * *

Meditating the first seven verses of St. John's Gospel

I.

Mornings: First seven verses of St. John's Gospel

In the primal beginning was the Word
And the Word was with God
And the Word was a God.
This was in the primal beginning with God.
There it was that all arose
And nothing arose
Other than through the Word.

In the light's pure rays
Expectant soul
Seek divine intimacy.

Evenings: Backward review

Divine intimacy
Seek expectant soul
In light's pure rays

(Peace of soul).

—Archive 6827

II.

Evenings: In the primal beginning was the Word
And the Word was with God
And the Word was a God.
And the Word
Lives in the heart,
In the heart of your essence,
In your "I."

Mornings: In your "I,"
In the heart of your essence,
Lives the Word,
The Spirit Word.
And the Word was with God,
And the Word was a God.
In the primal beginning was the Word.

—Archive 0062

III.

Evenings: In the primal beginning was Time's Word
And Time's Word was with God
And Time's Word was a God
And Time's Word
Lives in you.

Mornings: And Time's Word
Lives in me.
And Time's Word was a God
And Time's Word was with God;
In the primal beginning was Time's Word.

—Archive 6802

IV.

Evenings: 1. Backward Review (5–6 minutes)

         2. Meditation:
In the primal beginning was the Word
And may the Word be in me
And may the Word work in me
And may the Word bear me
Into Spirit Worlds
Into Soul Depths.

Mornings: Rose Cross—

May it be for me
The image of my self.
In my soul depths
Strong spirit forces
Like rose stars
On the black wood of the Cross.

—Archive A0066

V.

Evenings: Backward Review—from evening to morning (5 minutes)

Father
+
Holy Spirit

Through the Father all my life
Through Him also all my being
In the Son all my striving
In Life and also in death
Through the Spirit all truth
Of the heart and also the understanding
This I shall receive Light, Love, Life.

Mornings: All that is mine
From the divine
In Christ
I offer up all that is mine
And also life
So I shall awake
Now and in the future
In the Spirit of the World.

—Archive A0252

Various Christian meditations

Evenings: 1. Backward review
            2. Translation of St. John's Gospel into images
            3. Meditation:
                  In the primal beginning was the Word
                  And the Word was with God
                  And the Word was a God

Mornings: 1. Repetition of the images from the Evenings
            2. Meditation:
                  And may the Word be in me
                  And may the Word be in my soul
                  And may my will be out of the Word

—Archive 3157

Esoteric "Our Father"

For most of his life as an esoteric teacher, Rudolf Steiner prayed the
Lord's Prayer Standing upright, he used to say it so loudly in his Berlin
apartment that it could be heard in the neighboring room.

Father, you who were, are, and will be in our innermost being!
May your being be glorified and praised in us in all things.
May your kingdom grow in our deeds and our conduct.
May we perform your will in the activity of our lives, as you,
O Father, lay it down in our innermost soul.
You give us spiritual nourishment, the bread of life,
superabundantly in the changing conditions of our lives.
Let our mercy for others make up for the sins done to our being.
You do not allow the tempter to work in us beyond the capacity of
our strength, for in your being there can be no temptation; for the
tempter is but appearance and deception, from which you,
O Father, will safely lead us by the light of your knowledge.
May your power and glory work in us in all the cycles of time.

—Before 1913

At the end of his life, while he was being cared for by Ita Wegman, Rudolf Steiner prayed a slightly different version. J. E. Zeylmans von Emmichoven writes: "Ita Wegman watched as 'his physical strength gradually disappeared'. There were short times when he got up twice a day; then again his strength left him to such an extent that she had to support him when he wanted to pray. He recited the Lord's Prayer in a loud voice, standing upright every day, so that people passing by outside his studio heard him."

Father,
you who were, are, and will be
in our innermost being,
your name in us
is glorified and praised.

May your kingdom increase
in our deeds and our conduct.

May we perform your will,
as you, O Father, have laid it down
in our innermost being.

Spiritual nourishment, the bread of life,
you give us superabundantly
in all the changing conditions of our lives.

Let our mercy for others
balance the sins done to our being.

You do not allow the tempter to work in us
beyond the capacity of our strength.

For in your being, O Father, no temptation can exist,
for the tempter is but appearance and deception,
from which you, O Father,
will lead us by the light of your knowledge.

May your power and glory
work through us in all cycles of time.

The Gothic "Our Father"

When we try to translate this wonderful prayer from Wulfilas's language into our own contemporary languages, we cannot translate word for word, but must say something like this:

We sense You above in the heavenly heights,
All-Father of Humanity.
Consecrated be Your Name.
May your territory come.
May your will rule on Earth
As in Heaven.
All-Father, whose Name builds the Spirit's
Outer bodiliness, whose territory we
Wish to recognize, whose will should rule,
You should also permeate the earthly,
So that we see our bodies newly rise daily
As it were through earthly food.
That in social life we do not become guilty
One for another, that we face each other
Like equals, that we do not
Decay with the spiritual-physical.
Let us not decay into that which brings our Spirit
Into darkness out of our bodies, but deliver us from the Evils
That arise when we let our Spirit decay too strongly into the body.
Yours is the claim of Lordship, Yours is the right of Might,
Yours is the revelation as Light, as Shine,
As all-powerful social Love.

—May 15, 1921

The macrocosmic "Our Father"

The origins of this verse—the so-called "macrocosmic Lord's prayer"—lay in Steiner's spiritual research into the Christian Mystery. In his lectures on The Fifth Gospel, the so-called "Gospel of Knowledge," he told how the young Jesus came to understand that the Bath-Kol, the mysterious prophetic voice of inspiration issuing from the spirit of Yahweh himself, had grown weak. It could no longer inspire humanity as it had done before. The capacity to reach divine revelation had withdrawn. Realizing this, Jesus began his wanderings. Somewhere outside Palestine, he found himself before a "pagan" shrine. He was twenty-four. The people were wracked in misery and affliction. The priests had left. The sacrifices no longer worked. Recognizing in Jesus the expression of infinite love, the people impelled him toward the altar. Immediately, his soul was transported into the spiritual realms. He gazed into the depths of the human soul where all the suffering and grief of humanity was concentrated. As he did so, he felt himself lifted into the sphere of the Sun. There he heard the voice of wisdom of the Bath-Kol, but transformed. The sense of the words that Jesus heard became the cosmic prayer with which Steiner sealed the foundation stone of the first Goetheanum. He claimed that uttering this prayer of knowledge of the evils that accompany the liberation of the "I" and its separation from the spiritual world was "one of the most sublime moments of my experience in the course of our movement."

AUM,
AMEN.

Evils reign

Bearing witness to I-being
Separating itself
and to selfhood's guilt—
Incurred through others,
Experienced in the daily bread
Wherein the will of heaven
Does not reign,
Because humanity
Has separated itself
From Your kingdom
And forgot your names

Ye Fathers in the Heavens.

How do I find the Christ?

The Experience of Powerlessness & the Experience of Resurrection

We end this section with an instance of Rudolf Steiner's profound understanding of the Christ and the experiences leading to knowing Christ. The lecture is full and, as always, deep, multifaceted, and continuously interesting. The only reference requiring explanation is Steiner's reference (below) to "disease." To understand this we need only note that Steiner began by speaking of a threefold inclination of the human soul in relation to the divine spiritual Trinity of Father, Son, and Holy Spirit. Modernity according to Steiner is generally marked by a denial of these three. Steiner begins by characterizing this denial. To deny God the Father, the ground of all being, he calls an actual, physical disease; to deny Christ, he calls "a misfortune": to deny the Holy Spirit, "a dullness of one's spirit." In the course of his lecture, Steiner then connects this denial with the great event that occurred between the sixth and ninth centuries and culminated in the West with the reduction of the human being from a threefold being (of body, soul, and spirit) to a stark duality of body and soul. This, he says, "constitutes an internal injury, which sends its effects right down into the bodily constitution.... It is a disease instilled into humanity which, if acute, leads to the denial of God the Father."

... The following experience is important. If you have experienced it, you can find the Christ. First, you experience saying to yourself, "I shall strive for self-knowledge as far as it is possible for me to do so as an individual human personality."

But anybody who honestly strives as a human being today for self-knowledge will have to confess, "I cannot grasp what I am actually striving for. My power of comprehension lags far behind my striving. I experience *my powerlessness* in relation to my striving."

This is a most important experience. A certain feeling of powerlessness is an experience all those must have who, in self-knowledge, honestly and inwardly ponder things. This feeling of powerlessness is healthy. For it is nothing but the sensation of a disease. And we are truly ill, only to the extent that we have a disease and do not know it. By realizing our powerlessness to raise ourselves to the divine at any time in our life, we feel a disease implanted in us. Feeling this disease, we feel that the soul is condemned to die with the body as the body is condemned to die today.

If we feel this powerlessness strongly enough, transformation comes.

Then another experience follows. This one says, "If you do not devote yourself solely to what you can gain through your bodily forces, but devote yourself rather to what the spirit gives you, then you may be able to overcome this soul death."

We *can find* our soul again and join it to the spirit. If we transcend the feeling of powerlessness, we can experience both the nothingness of existence on the one hand and its glorification out of ourselves on the other. We feel in our powerlessness both the disease and the Healer, the healing power. We do so if we have felt our powerlessness which has become related to death in our souls. When we feel the Healer, we feel that we bear something in our souls that can rise from death *at any time* in our own inner experience.

If we seek these two experiences, we find the Christ in our own souls. This is an experience that humanity is approaching. Angelus Silesius stated it, when he wrote:

The Cross of Golgotha cannot redeem you
From evil so long as it remains unraised within you.

The Cross may be raised within us when we feel the two poles: *powerlessness* through our body, *resurrection* through our spirit.

The inner experience, consisting of these two parts, is what the Mystery of Golgotha actually intends. We cannot excuse ourselves from understanding the Mystery of Golgotha simply by saying we have not developed supersensible faculties. We do not need them. We need exercise only real self-reflection, as well as the will for it, and the will to struggle against pride—that pride, which is common

today, that prevents us from seeing that we become proud of our
own forces the moment we depend upon them. If, with regard to our
own pride, we cannot feel that we have become powerless through
our own forces, we are then unable to feel either death or resurrection. Then we shall never experience what Angelus Silesius says:

> The Cross of Golgotha cannot redeem you
> From evil, so long as it remains unraised within you.

If we can truly experience powerlessness and recovery from it,
then we can have the great good fortune of having a real relationship with the Christ Jesus. For this experience is the repetition of
what we experienced centuries before in the spirit world. Now we
must search for it in its reflected image in our soul on the physical
plane. Search yourselves, and you will find powerlessness. Having
found it, you will find redemption from it—the resurrection of
the soul by the spirit.

Do not let yourselves be misled by what is preached today as
mysticism or by theologians. If Harnack, for example, speaks of
the Christ, his statements are not true, for the simple reason that
what he says about the Christ may be said of God in general.
What he says may just as well be said of the God of Jews, or the
God of the Mohammedans, indeed, of every God. Many people
who today claim to be awakened say: I experience God within me.
But they only experience God the Father in a very weakened form,
because they do not perceive that they are ill, but merely base their
words on tradition. Such people do not experience Christ; for the
Christ-experience is not just realizing God in the soul. It consists
of two experiences—the death of the soul through the body, and
the resurrection of the soul through the spirit. Only those who
tell us that they not only feel the God within them, as merely rhe-
torical Theosophists also claim, but can also describe the two
experiences—powerlessness and resurrection from it—only
those describe the true Christ experience. Such people will find
their way to the Mystery of Golgotha on a supersensible path;

they will find the strength that stimulates certain supersensible forces and that lead one to the Mystery of Golgotha.

Therefore there is no need to give up hope of finding the Christ in our direct personal experience. If we have recovered ourselves from powerlessness, we have found Him. The whole feeling of nothingness, of futility, which comes over us when we, without pride, ponder over our own forces, has to precede the Christ impulse. Clever mystics believe they possess Christianity when they are able to say: I have found within my "I" the higher "I," God's "I." But this is not Christianity. Christianity must be based upon the sentence:

The Cross of Golgotha cannot redeem you
From evil, so long as it remains unraised within you.

—October 16, 1918

Working with the Dead

For many years, Rudolf Steiner gave out many meditations and practices to help those on Earth remain connected to those who have died. Practices include:

Reading to the dead:

It is clearly not a case of the dead understanding any particular human language—English, French, or Swahili. The essence of what is read must become living spiritual thinking in us. We must start with a spiritual text; we thoroughly ponder and make it our own; then, to the best of our ability, we, as it were, meditate it to the highest "meaning." Then, emptying ourselves, we offer this experience to the spiritual world and, specifically, to our loved one who has died.

Remembering the dead:

In the first place, this means thinking of the dead, summoning them before us, with as much life and accuracy and as great and pure a love as we can muster. We must learn to love objectively, not out of personal need. The souls of the dead need nourishment, just as we need food. Thoughts filled with heart and love become food for those who have died. Steiner says that we are "books" for those who have gone over to the other side. They hunger for the spiritual knowledge we can gain only on Earth. Our memory of them is "art" for them. If we wish to communicate with them, a useful exercise to create them in memory and then, as selflessly and unegotistically as we can, enter into their image so totally that we become them.

Working with images and thoughts:

Those who have died sometimes appear to us as images—often not in their own likeness, but in the image of another person or thing. This image is, as it were, the gaze of the loved one upon us. We can also feel the individual's presence and gaze as thoughts that come as if by grace. We must try to become sensitive to the presence of this "other" in our thought life—for the dead wish to help in the work of earthly evolution.

Questioning those who have died:

This is best done last thing at night before falling asleep. As we go to sleep, we turn with a question, in pure love and deep feeling, to the one who passed away. The question is carried in the heart into sleep. Awaking the next morning, we pay close attention to the first thing in our consciousness. This answer will be in our own voice, not that of the other.

Steiner also spoke of certain preconditions:

- We must learn to understand that Earth is the place for creating connections and relationships that can be continued after death. The meaning of the Earth is relationship.

- We must learn to develop a moral disposition that acknowledges the unity and ultimate value of all human beings. This begins with developing an interest in and love for everyone we meet.

- We must learn to cultivate a feeling of devotion and reverence.

- We must always seek to unite with the presence of the ever-present universal spirit and thereby establish the common, spiritual ground that the living and the dead share. We must learn to develop "inner quiet," emptying ourselves and waiting for thoughts, feelings, and insights to arise from the soul's depths. This is the "inward" side." Outwardly, we must begin to pay attention to chance encounters and synchronicities—to the events around us.

- We must seek to acquire a sense of "community," or "solidarity," with all life and all that exists. We must realize that we are part of the world; we leave our mark on all that we encounter and remain connected with everything we come into contact with. We are part of the web of Earth; we can no longer live for ourselves alone.

- We must learn to develop a sense of gratitude, a feeling of universal gratitude for all the experiences of life. We are given everything. Everything is a gift.

- We must learn to develop "trust in life." Whatever happens, "Life, you lift and bear me; you make certain that I move forward."

Rudolf Steiner also gave specific meditations and indications to various individuals in particular circumstances. Adapted, they are of universal application. Here are a few of them.

May my love *be* for you
In the spirit realm.
May my seeking soul
Find your soul.
May *my* thinking of *your* being
Ease your cold,
Ease your heat.
In this way, we shall be united:
I with you,
You with me.

—No date

In the light
Of cosmic thoughts
The soul weaves
That unites with me on Earth.

—Notebook entry, 1924

To bind soul to soul,
I shall send the faithful love
We found
Into the fields of spirit.
If you turn your soul
From the lands of spirit light,
Seeking to see what you seek in me,
You will find my thinking
Through love.

—Notebook entry, 1916

In the worlds
Where the kernel
Of your being's soul
Now sojourns,
I send *love* to you—
To cool your heat,
To warm your coldness.
If you find me in *feeling*
I shall always be near you.

—No date

May my heart-love reach to soul love,
May my love's warmth shine to spirit light.
Thus, I draw near to you,
Thinking spiritual thoughts *with* you,
Feeling cosmic love *in* you,
Willing in spirit *through* you—
Weaving with you
One in experience.

—To Rudolf Hahn, for his wife,
Marie, September 1918

May my heart's warm life
Stream to your soul,
To warm your coldness,
To soothe your heat.
May *my* thoughts live in *your* thoughts—
And your thoughts in my thoughts—
In the spiritual worlds.

—Notebook entry, 1924

May my soul's love *strive* to you,
May my love's meaning *stream* to you,
May they *bear* you,
May they *hold* you,
In the heights of *hope*,
In the spheres of *love*.

—No date

May our love follow you,
O soul,
Living there in spirit,
Seeing your earthly life,
Seeing yourself cognized as spirit.
And what appears to you
In the land of souls to be yourself,
Thinking—
Accept our love
So that we may feel ourselves in you
And you may find in *our* souls
What lives with you in faithfulness.

—For the death of Marie Hahn,
September 1918

I see you
In the spiritual world
Where you are.
May my love
Alleviate your heat,
Alleviate your cold.
It breaks through to you
And helps you
To find the way
Through the spirit's darkness
To the spirit's light.

—No date

As the golden stars shine forth
From the blue depths of spirit,
So from my depths of my soul
The strong upholding powers stream forth.
[accompanied by a drawing: yellow stars on a blue background]

—To Hermine Stein, on the death of her son
Friedrich in battle, March 22, 1915

Faithfully,
I will follow your soul
Through the gate of death
Into the light-engendering
time-places—
With *love*, I will ease spirit coldness for you,
With *knowing*, I will untangle spirit light for you,
With *thinking*, I will linger with you.

—For Gertrud Noss, on the death of her son
Fritz Mitscher, February 1915

May my soul follow you
Into the realm of spirit,
Follow you with the same love
It was able to nurture
In the realm of Earth
When my eye could still behold you,
May it ease your warmth, ease your cold—
Thus we live united,
Unseparated, through the door of spirit.

        —For Gertrud Noss, on the death of her son
                Fritz Mitscher, February 1915

Feel how we gaze lovingly
Into heights that now
Call you to other work.
May your power reach out
From spirit-realms
To the friends you left behind.

Hear our souls' request
Sent to you in confidence:
We need here, for our earthly work,
Strong power from spirit lands—
We thank our friends now dead for this.

A hope that makes us happy,
A loss that pains us deeply,
Let us hope that you light our lives,
Far-and-near, unlost,
A soul-star in the spiritual firmament.

        —For Fritz Mitscher, February 5, 1915

May my soul follow you into the spiritual realm,
Follow you with that love
You were permitted to preserve in the earthly realm
As my eyes still saw you
May cold relieve you, may warm relieve you
So let us live united
Unseparated through the Gate of Spirit.

—On the death of Gertud Noss, September 1915

1. Your will was weak
2. Strengthen your will
3. I send you
    Warmth for your cold
4. I send you
    Light for your darkness
5. My love to you
6. My thoughts to you
7. Go — become — further.

—To Franz Gerner, for a friend
lost through suicide, no date

You were ours
And you will be ours
As the light of the spirit
Now streams from your soul eyes
Filled with devotion.

It will be your thoughts'
Noble power
To seek in spirit worlds
The love that faithfully
We keep for you.

—Notebook entry, 1917

O Soul in the land of soul
Seek Christ's grace
That brings you aid,
Aid from spirit lands,
And gives peace
To those spirits
Who, experiencing no peace,
Want to despair.

　　　　　—For a mother whose son took his life

Companion of my life,
Help the steps,
My thoughts,
Go to you,
To bring them to him,
I ask your soul, my spouse—

　　　　　　—To the same mother, for her
　　　　　　　　deceased husband, no date

You never set me apart
From what you have given me
To love;
Your spirit guards mine
For it is yours also;
So I will guard with you,
Through you, in you,
What you have agreed
With those who are yours—
I will be strong, and know
That it is wisdom.

　　　　　　—For Mrs. Roemer, after the death
　　　　　　　　of her son, Christmas 1919

May the eyes of your soul look
Into my thoughts' deeper power—
That is my will.
May my will meet your will
in the Father's power
in the Son's grace
in the Spirit's light.
—For William Scott Pyle after
the death of Edith Maryon

My thoughts stream
Heartwarming
Into your soul's sleep.
Experience them in your "I"
Now free.
I will be with you.
And bring out of your life,
From earthly existence,
What you need for spirit remembering.
—For Margaret Bockholt, after the
death of her father, January 1924

With you, my soul
Seeks you, intuitively
My soul is with you
And lives your task
With you.
Thus we are
United karmically
For all time.
—For Gertrud and Wilhelm von Heydebrand
after the short life of a child, c.1912

To you
In love
On Christ's Ways
Seek my heart
Live
In my thoughts
As I live in your soul.

—To a mother after the death of her
small child, June 1921

Divinity in my soul,
I will give you space
In my conscious being;
You connect me to all
That the power of destiny brings me.

In the beginning was the Word
And I myself was in the Word
And the Word was in God.
With the Word I myself was in God
And the Word was a God.
And a God saw me in the Word
And the Word should live in my soul.

—For M. Corre, at the death of his father, no date

* * *

Looking up into the spiritual worlds, we see there what were once human acts—having passed through the Angels, Archangels, Archai (Principalities), Exusiai (Powers), Dynamis (Virtues), and Kiriotetes (Dominions)—received by the Thrones, Cherubim, and Seraphim, expanding as their heavenly acts above.

[Therefore we may pray]

Angels, Archangels, Principalities, receive our beloved's web of destiny into your etheric weaving.
In Powers, Virtues, Dominions—in the astral feeling of the cosmos—the righteous consequences of our beloved's earthly life die away.
In Thrones, Cherubim, and Seraphim the justly transformed fruits of our beloved's earthly life are resurrected.

—Lecture, July 4, 1924

Coda: the dead speak

I am not on Earth as soul
but only in water, air, and fire;

In my fire I am in the planets
and the Sun.

In my sun-being I am the
sky of the fixed stars —

I am not on the Earth as soul
but in Light, Word, and Life;

In my life I am within
the being of the sun and the planets, in the Spirit
of Wisdom.

In my wisdom being I am in the
Spirit of Love.

—Notebook entry, New Year 1917/1918

No barrier can separate
What, united in the spirit,
Preserves
The light-shining
Love-streaming
Eternal soul bond;
Thus I am in your thoughts
Thus may you be in mine.

—Sketch

I was united with you,
Remain united in me.
We shall speak together
In the language of eternal being.
We will be active
Where actions become events,
We will weave in the Spirit
Where human thoughts are woven
In the Word of eternal Thoughts.

—Address for Georga Wiese, January 11, 1924

The Foundation Stone Meditation

At the center of Anthroposophy, as its lifeblood and heart, lies this meditation, which Rudolf Steiner laid "in the hearts of the members" at the first meeting of the reconstituted General Anthroposophical Society during the Holy Nights of 1923–24. It represents the seed and the fruit of anthroposophic striving—the seed, because meditating upon it develops the full and glorious being of Anthroposophia; the fruit, because it is the culmination of Steiner's spiritual work.

Human soul!
You live in the limbs
that carry you through the world of space
into Spirit's ocean being.
Practice *spirit recollection*
in the soul's depths,
where, in the powerful
world creator's being,
your "I" gains being
in the "I" of God;
then, you will truly *live*
in human cosmic being.

For the Father spirit of the heights reigns
in the world's depths, begetting being.
Spirits of power,
let what echoes in the depths

ring out from the heights,
saying:
Humanity's being is born from the Divine.
Spirits hear this in the east, west, north, south.
May human beings hear it.

Human soul!
You live in the beat of heart and lung,
which leads you through time's rhythm
into the feeling of your own soul's being.
Practice *spirit awareness*
in serenity of soul,
where surging
deeds of world becoming
unite your "I"
with the "I" of the world;
then, you shall truly *feel*
in the soul's inner working.

For the Christ will reigns in the spheres around us,
shedding grace upon souls in the world's rhythms.
Spirits of light,
let what is formed in the west
be kindled from the east,
saying:
In Christ, death becomes life.

Spirits hear this in east, west, north, south.
May human beings hear it!

Human soul!
You live in the silence of the head,
where from eternal foundations
cosmic thoughts unveil before you:

Practice *spirit beholding*
in peace of thought,
where for your free willing
the gods' eternal aims
shed cosmic being's light
on your innermost "I";
then you will truly *think*
in the foundations of the human spirit.

For Spirit's cosmic thoughts reign
In the world's being, beseeching light.
Spirits of soul
let what is heard in the heights
be sought in the depths,
saying
The soul awakens in Spirit's cosmic thinking.

Spirits hear this in east, west, north, south.
May human beings hear it.

At the turn of time,
cosmic spirit light descended
into the Earth's stream of being.
Night's darkness
had run its course.
Day-bright light
streamed into human souls—
light
that warms
poor shepherds' hearts;
light
that illumines
the wise heads of kings.

Divine light,
Christ Sun,
warm through
our hearts,
illumine
our heads
so that what
we would create
from our hearts
and guide from our heads,
in sure willing,
may be good.

Meeting the Guardians

Central to the spiritual work on inner development is what Rudolf Steiner calls (following Bulwer Lytton, who introduced the term in his Rosicrucian novel Zanoni) the "Meeting with the Guardian of the Threshold." Although a great deal could and ought to be said of this pivotal spiritual experience, the following passages from How to Know Higher Worlds are more or less self-explanatory and must suffice.

The Lesser Guardian

Among the most important experiences in the ascent to higher worlds are the encounters with the so-called *guardian of the threshold*. Actually, there are two such beings, not one. They are known as the "lesser" and the "greater" guardians. We meet the first when the connection between willing, thinking, and feeling in the finer (astral and ether) bodies begins to loosen. The second, greater guardian is encountered when the separation of these three forces also affects the physical body, particularly the brain.

The lesser guardian of the threshold is an independent being, who does not exist for us until we have reached the appropriate level of inner development. Within the framework of this book, therefore, only a brief description of this guardian's essential characteristics is given.

First, an attempt will be made to give a narrative description of the meeting with this guardian. It is only through this meeting, in fact, that we become aware that the implanted connection between thinking, feeling, and willing has been undone.

A thoroughly horrid, ghostly being stands before us. Hence we shall need full presence of mind and complete confidence in the safety and reliability of our cognitive path—which we have had ample opportunity to acquire in the course of our training—for this encounter.

The guardian then reveals the meaning of this moment in words, somewhat as follows:

Up to now, unseen by you, mighty powers presided over you. Through all the previous courses of your lives, they brought it about that every good deed was followed by its reward, and every evil action was followed by its grievous consequences. Through their influence your character was formed out of your life experiences and thoughts. They were the agents of your destiny. They determined, on the basis of your conduct in previous lives, the measure of joy and pain allotted to you in each of your incarnations. They ruled over you in the form of the all-embracing law of karma. These powers will now begin to loosen the reins by which they guide you. Now you yourself must do some of the work they did for you before.

Up to now, you endured many heavy blows of fate. You did not know why. Each was the consequence of a damaging deed done in a previous life. You found joy and happiness, and took these as you found them. These, too, were the result of earlier actions. You have many beautiful sides to your character, and many ugly flaws. You yourself produced these through your past experiences and thoughts. Up to now, you were unaware of this; only the effects were known to you. But the karmic powers witnessed all your former actions and even your most secret thoughts and feelings. And on that basis they determined who you are now and how you live in your present incarnation.

Now, however, all the good and bad aspects of your past lives are to be revealed to you. You will see them for yourself.

They have been interwoven with your being all along. They were in you, and you could not see them, just as you cannot see your brain with your eyes. Now, however, your past actions are separating themselves from you, stepping out of your personality. They are assuming an independent form, one that you can see, as you can see the stones and plants of the outside world. I am that selfsame being, who made a body for itself out of your good and your wicked deeds. My ghostly form is spun, so to speak, from the account book of your life. Up to now, you have carried me invisibly within you. It was for your sake that this was so. It meant that the hidden wisdom of your destiny continued to work within you to eliminate the ugly spots in my appearance. Now that I have come forth from you, this hidden wisdom has also left you and will take care of you no longer. Instead, it puts the work into your own hands. I myself, if I am not to fall into corruption, must become a perfect and glorious being. For, were I to fall, I would drag you down with me into a dark, corrupted world.

To prevent this, your own wisdom must be great enough to take over the task previously performed by the hidden wisdom now departed from you. I shall never leave your side once you have crossed my threshold. I shall always be there beside you in a form you can perceive. From then on, whenever you think or act wrongly, you will immediately see your fault as an ugly, demonic distortion in my appearance. My being will be changed and become radiantly beautiful only when you have made amends for all your wrongs and have so purified yourself that you become incapable of further evil. Then, too, I shall be able to unite with you again as a single being in order to bless and benefit your further activity.

My threshold is built of every feeling of fear still within you and every feeling of reluctance in the face of the strength you need to take on full responsibility for your thoughts and actions. As long as you still harbor any trace of fear at directing your own destiny, the threshold lacks an essential element. As long as a single stone is missing, you will remain on this threshold, as if spellbound—or stumble. Therefore, do not try to cross this threshold until you are completely free of fear and feel yourself ready for the highest responsibility.

Until now, I have left you only when death called you from an earthly life. But, even then, my form was veiled from your eyes. Only the powers of destiny presiding over you could see me. During the interval between death and rebirth, based on my appearance, they formed in you the forces and faculties to enable you to work to make me beautiful in your next life, and so ensure the well-being of your progress. Thus it was I and my imperfections that made the powers of destiny send you back to a new earthly incarnation. When you died, I was there. It was for my sake that the rulers of karma decided that you must reincarnate. If, without knowing it, you were to transform and perfect me through life forever renewed in this way, then you could avoid falling into the powers of death. But then you would have become completely one with me, and, united, we would pass into immortality.

Now I stand visible before you, as I have always stood invisible beside you in the hour of your death. Once you have crossed my threshold, you will enter realms you otherwise entered only after physical death. Now you will enter them in full knowledge. From now on, though living outwardly and visibly upon the Earth, you will live at the same time in the realm of death, that is, in the realm of eternal life. Indeed, I am your angel of death. At the same time I also bring you never-ending higher life. While still living in the body, you will die through me and experience rebirth into indestructible existence.

In the realm you are henceforth entering, you will meet beings of a suprasensory kind. Bliss will be your share in this realm. Yet I, I who am your own creation, must be your first acquaintance in this world. Earlier, I lived on your life. But now, through you, I have awakened to an independent existence of my own and stand before you as the visible standard of your future actions—and perhaps also as a constant reproach. You have been able to create me and in so doing have taken on the duty of transforming me.

What is indicated here in narrative form must not be understood only symbolically. It is, on the contrary, in the highest degree an absolutely real experience, which any student pursuing esoteric training to the appropriate level can have.

The guardian's function is to warn us not to go any further unless we feel strong enough to meet the challenges contained in the words addressed to us. Horrid as it may be, the guardian's appearance is, after all, but the consequence of our own past lives. It is only our own character, awakened to an independent life outside of us.

This awakening of our character to an independent existence occurs as our thinking, willing, and feeling begin to separate. It is already a deeply meaningful experience to feel for the first time that we have given birth to a spiritual being. The whole purpose of our preparation—our esoteric training—is to enable us to bear the awful sight of this guardian without any trace of fear or aversion. When we meet the guardian we must feel our strength so grown that we can take upon ourselves the task of the guardian's transformation and enhancement in full knowledge and consciousness.

As a result of passing the meeting with the guardian of the threshold successfully, our next physical death is a quite different event than before. Dying becomes a conscious experience for us in which we lay aside our physical body, like a garment that is worn out or so torn that it is no longer usable. In a sense, our physical death will then upset only those close to us whose outlook and perceptions are still limited to the material world. In their eyes we "die," but nothing important changes for us in our surroundings. For before we die the whole suprasensory world that we enter with death is already open to us—and after dying it remains open to us as before.

The guardian of the threshold is also connected with something else. Each of us belongs to a family, a people, a race. Our activity in this world depends upon our belonging to such a unit. Even our individual personality is related to it. In fact, our membership in a family, a nation, or a race affects not only our conscious activities, for every family, nation, and race has its own destiny, just as each has its own particular character. As long as our perspective is limited to the material world, however, such realities remain merely general concepts. Materialistically biased thinkers regard with contempt any esoteric scientist who attributes family or national characteristics and lineal or racial destinies to beings whom they consider just as real as the individuality to whom they attribute personality and destiny. Yet such esoteric scientists have come to know *worlds* of which our individual personalities are parts, just as our arms, legs, and head are parts of our body.

The life of families, nations, and races is affected thus not only by the individuals who belong to them but also by "family souls," "nation souls," and "race spirits." These are real beings. In a sense, as individuals, we are only the instruments—the executive organs, so to speak—of these "family souls" and "race spirits." Indeed we may say, for example, that the soul of a nation or people makes use of the individuals who belong to it to accomplish certain tasks. This "folk soul" does not descend to the sense-perceptible world: it remains in the higher realms. To work in the physical world, the folk soul of a nation makes use of individual human beings as physical organs. This process is analogous, on a higher level, to a civil engineer in the material world making use of construction workers to execute the details of a project.

In the truest sense, we each receive our allotted human task from our family, nation, or race soul. As long as our experience is limited to the sense-perceptible world, we are not initiated into the higher purpose of which this task is a part, but work unconsciously toward the goals of our group souls. As soon as we encounter the guardian of the threshold, however, we not only know our own personal tasks but also have to work consciously to help accomplish those of our people and our race. Thus, each expansion of our horizon also extends the sphere of our responsibility.

The actual process underlying this revelation at the threshold is the adding of a new body to our subtler body. This is much like putting on a new garment. Previously we moved through the world clothed only in the sheaths that envelop our personality. Higher spirits, making use of our personality, oversaw what we had to do for our community, our nation, and our race. Now, however, the guardian of the threshold reveals to us that these spirits will no longer take care of us—from now on they withdraw their guiding hands. We must therefore leave behind all belonging to communities. Yet, as isolated individuals, we would wholly harden within ourselves and fall into ruin if we did not acquire the powers inherent in the spirits of our race and nation.

While many people certainly believe they have freed themselves fully from all tribal and racial connections and are simply "human" and nothing else, we have to wonder what made this freedom possible for them. After all, were they not given their place in the world by their family, and have not their lineage, nation, and race made them what they are? Their lineage, nation, and race have taught and educated them. They owe their ability to transcend tribal and racial prejudices to this education; lineage, nation, and race have enabled them to become the light-bearers and benefactors of their tribe or even their race. Thus, even though these people claim to be no more than "simply human," they owe the ability to make such claims to the spirits of their communities. In fact, only when we follow the path to inner knowledge will we experience what it really means to have left behind all tribal, national, and racial connections and to be abandoned by the spirits of nation, tribe, and race.

Indeed, it is on the esoteric path that we first experience for ourselves the meaninglessness of the education—for the life we are now entering—that all these connections have given us. For as soon as the threads joining willing, thinking, and feeling begin to snap, all that has been instilled in us completely dissolves. We then look back upon the results of our previous upbringing as if we were watching our house crumble into individual bricks that we must then rebuild in a new form.

It is much more than a mere figure of speech when we are told that, after the guardian begins to speak, a whirlwind arises from the place where the guardian stands, extinguishing all the spiritual lights that illuminated our life up to now. Utter darkness then surrounds us, broken only by the radiance streaming from the guardian. Out of this darkness we hear the guardian exhorting us: *Do not cross my threshold until you fully understand that you yourself have to illuminate the darkness before you. Do not take a single step forward until you are absolutely sure that you have enough fuel in your own lamp—because the lamps of those who have guided you up to now will no longer be there in the future.*

Following these words, we must turn and cast our gaze behind us. The guardian of the threshold now pulls aside the curtain that hitherto veiled life's deep mysteries from us. Now the spirits of tribe, nation, and race are revealed in their full reality. We see clearly how we have been guided in the past and that now this guidance is no more. This is the second warning we receive at the threshold from its guardian.

No one could bear the sight described here without preparation. The higher training that enables us to reach the threshold helps us at the same time to find the necessary strength when we need it. In fact, our training can proceed so harmoniously that when we enter this new life we do so without drama or tumult. Our experiences at the threshold are then accompanied by a premonition of that bliss which will be the keynote of our newly awakened life. The sensation of our new freedom outweighs all other feelings. And in the light of this sensation, our new duties and responsibilities seem natural and inevitable at our given stage of life.

The Greater Guardian

We have showed that the significance of the encounter with the so-called lesser guardian of the threshold lies in the fact that in this meeting we perceive a suprasensory being that we ourselves have, to some extent, created. For the body of this being is made up of the results—previously invisible to us—of our own actions, feelings, and thoughts. Unbeknownst to us, these invisible powers became the causes of our destiny and personality. And from this moment on, we realize how we ourselves laid the foundations of our present life in the past. In this way, our own being begins to become transparent to us.

For example, certain tendencies and habits live within us. Now, we realize why we have these. We have met with certain strokes of fate. Now, we recognize where these come from. We understand why we love some things and hate others, why some things make us happy and others cause us unhappiness. That is, we come to understand our visible life on the basis of its invisible causes. Even the essential facts of life, such as illness and health, birth and death, are unveiled before our sight. We realize that we wove the causes that led us to return to life before we were born. We come to know, too, the being within us that is created but unfinished in this visible world—the being that can be finished and perfected only in this same visible, perceptible world. For the opportunity to work on the completion of this being does not exist in any world other than this.

Thus we recognize that death cannot permanently separate us from this world. Inwardly, we realize: "Once I entered this world for the first time because I am a being who needs life in this world in order to acquire qualities I cannot acquire in any other world. And I must remain connected to this world until I have developed everything within me that can be found there. One day, because I have acquired all the faculties I need in this sense-perceptible, visible world I shall become a useful coworker in another world."

In other words, one of the most important experiences we gain from initiation is that we learn to know and to treasure the true value of the visible, sense-perceptible world better than we could before our esoteric training. Indeed, only through insight into the suprasensory worlds do we realize the value of the sense-perceptible world. A person who has not experienced this insight and thus perhaps believes that the suprasensory regions are of infinite, incomparable worth, may underestimate the sense-perceptible world. But those who have had insight into the suprasensory know that without their experiences in the visible world they would be quite powerless in the invisible worlds.

To live in the invisible worlds, we must have the tools and faculties appropriate to them. We can develop these only in the visible world. For example, if we are to become aware of the invisible worlds, we must learn to "see" spiritually. This power of spiritual vision in a "higher" world develops only gradually by means of experiences in the "lower" world. A person who has not previously developed these eyes in the sensible world can just as little be born with spiritual eyes in a spiritual world as a child could be born with physical eyes if these had not been developed in the mother's body.

We can now understand why the "threshold" to the suprasensory world is protected by a guardian. For under no circumstances could we be allowed a true insight into these realms if we had not first developed the necessary faculties. And this is the reason why, if we have not yet developed the ability to work in other worlds, a veil is drawn across our experiences when we die and enter these realms. That is, we may not behold the suprasensory worlds until we are ready and mature enough to do so.

When we enter the suprasensory worlds, life takes on a completely new meaning for us. We see that the sensible world is the fertile soil—the living medium or substratum—of a higher world. Indeed, in a certain sense, this "higher" world seems incomplete without the "lower" one. Two vistas then open up before us—one into the past, the other into the future. We see into a past in which this physical, sensible world did not yet exist. The prejudice that the suprasensory spiritual world developed out of the sensible material world lies far behind us now. We know that the suprasensory world came first and that the sensible physical world developed out of it.

At this point, our vision turns toward the future, revealing a higher level of the suprasensory world. Here we find fruits first formed in the sense-perceptible physical world. The sense world we know today will have been overcome by then, but its results will have been incorporated into a higher world. We see that before we entered the physical world for the first time we ourselves belonged to a supersensible world, and that this supersensible world too had to pass through life in the sensible world in order to develop further. Its further evolution was impossible unless it passed through the physical realm. Indeed, only if certain beings evolved with the appropriate faculties in the physical realm could the supersensible realm advance in its evolution. We are those beings. Human beings, as we are today, arise at a level of spiritual existence that is incomplete, imperfect. Within this level we are in the process of being led to a stage of completion that will enable us to continue our work in the higher world.

We can now begin to understand the meaning of illness and death in the physical world. Death, after all, merely expresses the fact that the supersensible world had previously reached a point beyond which it could not advance by its own efforts. Universal death would have overtaken it if it had not received a new life-impulse. This new life has become a struggle against universal death. Out of the ruins of a withering, inwardly solidifying world, the buds of a new world blossomed. That is why our world contains both death and life—and why things are gradually intermingling. The dying parts of the old world still cling to the seeds of the new life developing out of them. We can see this most clearly expressed in ourselves. The sheath we bear has been preserved from the old world, but the seed of the being that will live in the future is already growing within it.

Hence, as human beings we have a double nature: mortal and immortal. Our mortal being is in its final stages, our immortal being is only beginning. But only within the twofold world, mortal and immortal, whose expression is the sense-perceptible physical world, can we acquire the faculties that will lead the world to immortality. Our task is to harvest from the mortal world fruits for the immortal. When we contemplate our being, which we ourselves have built up in the past, we must say to ourselves: "We bear within ourselves the elements of a dying world. These elements work within us. Yet gradually, with the help of the new immortal elements awakening within us, we are able to break their power." In this way, our path takes us from death to life.

Indeed, if we were conscious in the hour of our death, we would realize: "The dying world was our teacher. The fact that we die is a result of all the past with which we are interwoven. But the field of mortality has prepared seeds of immortality for us. We carry these with us into another world. If everything depended only on the past, we would never have been born. The past—its life—ends with birth. Life in the sensible world is wrested from universal death by the new seed of life. The time between birth and death is simply an expression of how much the new life can wring from the dying past. And illness is but the consequence of the part of this past that is dying."

Here we find an answer to the question, "Why must we work our way only gradually from error and imperfection to truth and goodness?" Our actions, feelings, and thoughts begin under the rulership of what passes and dies away. Out of what passes away, our perceptible physical organs evolve and are fashioned. As a result, these organs and all that stimulates them are doomed to perish and die away. We will not therefore find anything immortal in our instincts, drives, and passions, nor in the organs belonging to them. We will find immortality only in what appears as their product, in the work done by these organs. Only when we have drawn out of this perishable world all that there is to be drawn out of it will we be able to cast aside the foundation we have outgrown, which manifests itself in the physical-sensible world.

Thus the first guardian of the threshold replicates our dual nature as human beings, consisting of mixed mortal and immortal elements. And thereby this guardian clearly reveals to us what still needs to be done to attain the sublime light form capable of dwelling again in the world of pure spirit.

The first guardian makes graphically clear how entangled we are with the physical, sensible world. This entanglement is expressed, first of all, by the presence of instincts, drives, passions, egotistic desires, and all forms of self-interest. It manifests, too, in our belonging to a race, a nation, and so forth. Peoples and races are, after all, merely different developmental stages in our evolution toward a pure humanity. The more perfectly that individual members of a race or people express the pure, ideal human type—the more they have worked their way through from the physical and mortal to the supersensible and immortal realm—the "higher" this race or nation is.

Human evolution, through repeated incarnations in ever "higher" nations and races, is thus a process of liberation. In the end, we must all appear in harmonious perfection. We perfect ourselves likewise as we pass through ever purer moral and religious convictions. For every stage of moral development still harbors some yearning for what is perishable, as well as idealistic seeds of the future.

What the lesser guardian of the threshold shows us are only the results of time that has passed. The seeds of the future are present only to the extent that they have been woven into the guardian in the past. But human beings are called upon to bring with them into the future supersensible world all that they can gain from the material world. Were we to bring with us only what was woven into our image from the past, we would accomplish only a part of our earthly task. That is why, after a certain period of time, the lesser guardian of the threshold is joined by a greater guardian. What takes place in the form of this meeting with the second, greater guardian will once again be described in narrative form.

After we have recognized in the lesser guardian those things from which we need to free ourselves, a magnificent form of light comes to meet us on the path. The beauty of this form is difficult to describe in ordinary language. The meeting takes place when our physical organs of thinking, feeling, and willing have so separated from each other—and even from the physical body—that they themselves no longer regulate their mutual interaction. Instead, higher consciousness, now detached completely from physical conditions, regulates their relations. As a result, our organs of thinking, feeling, and willing have become instruments under the control of the soul, which exercises its rulership from the supersensible realms. The soul, freed in this way from all sensory bonds, now encounters the second guardian of the threshold, who speaks somewhat as follows:

You have freed yourself from the world of the senses. You have earned the right of citizenship in the supersensible world. From now on, you may work from there. For yourself, you no longer need your physical bodily nature in its present form. If all you wanted was to acquire the capacity to dwell in the supersensible world, you would never need to return to the world of the senses. Look at me. See how immeasurably I am raised above all that you have already made of yourself up to now. You have reached your present stage of completion by means of faculties that you were able to develop in the sense world while you were still dependent upon it. Now you are entering a time when the powers you liberated must continue to work upon this sense world. Until now, you have worked only to free yourself, but now that you are free, you can help free all your fellow beings in the sense world. Up to now, you have striven as an individual. Now you must join yourself to the whole, so that you may bring with you into the supersensible realm not only yourself, but also all else that exists in the sensible world.

Someday, you will be able to unite with my form, but I myself cannot find perfect blessedness as long as there are others who are still unfortunate! As a single, liberated individual, you could enter the realm of the supersensible today. But then you would have to look down upon those sentient beings who are not yet freed. You would have separated your destiny from theirs. But you are linked together with all sentient beings. All of you had to descend into the world of the senses to draw from it the powers required for a higher world. Were you to separate yourself from your fellow beings, you would misuse the powers you were able to develop only in consort with them. If they had not descended into the sense world, you would not have been able to descend either. Without them, you would lack the powers you need for supersensible existence. You must share with the others the powers that you achieved with them.

Therefore I refuse to admit you to the highest regions of the supersensible world until you have used all your powers for the deliverance of your fellow world and fellow beings. What you have already achieved entitles you to dwell in the lower regions of the supersensible world. But I will stand at the doorway to the higher regions "like the cherubim with the flaming sword before the gates of Paradise." I will deny you entry as long as you still have powers that you have not put to use in the sense world.

If you do not use your own powers, others will come who will put them to use. Then a high supersensible world will incorporate all the fruit of the sensible realm, but the ground you stand on will be pulled out from under your feet. The purified world will develop over and beyond you. You will be excluded from it. If this is your choice, then yours is the black path. But those from whom you separate yourself tread the white path.

In this way the great guardian of the threshold announces his presence soon after the meeting with the first guardian. Initiates now know precisely what awaits those who yield to the temptations of a premature stay in the suprasensory realms. The second guardian of the threshold emits an indescribable radiance. Union with this guardian is a distant goal for the beholding soul. Yet the certainty is also present that such a union is possible only after all the powers that have flowed into us from this world have been expended in the service of liberating and redeeming it.

Should we therefore decide to meet the demands of this higher being of light, we will be able to contribute to the liberating of the human race. We will then offer up our gifts and talents on the sacrificial altar of humanity. But if we prefer our own premature ascent into the suprasensory world, then the stream of humanity will pass over and beyond us. Once we have liberated ourselves, we can no longer win any new powers for ourselves from the world of the senses. If, therefore, we still place our work at the disposal of the sense world, we do so knowing that we are thereby renouncing any gain for ourselves from the place of our future effort. But even when the choices are presented so clearly, it cannot be said that taking the white path is a matter of course. What we choose, after all, depends on whether we have sufficiently purified ourselves of all traces of selfishness, so that at the time of making the decision the allure of personal salvation and blessedness no longer tempts us.

This temptation of personal salvation on the "black" path is the greatest we can conceive of. The white path, on the other hand, does not seem tempting at all. It does not appeal to our egotism. What we receive in the higher regions of the supersensible realms when we take the white path is not something for ourselves, but only something that flows from us, namely, love for the world and our fellow beings around us. But on the black path nothing that our egotism desires is denied us. On the contrary, the fruit of this path is precisely the complete satisfaction of egotism. Thus those seeking salvation only for themselves will almost certainly choose the black path. In their case, indeed, it is appropriate.

Clearly, therefore, we must not expect esotericists on the white path to provide any instructions for the development of our egotistic "I." They have no interest whatsoever in the bliss and salvation of the individual. As far as a white occultist is concerned, each one of us must attain such salvation for ourselves. It is not their task to accelerate this process. What matters to them is the evolution and liberation of *all* beings—human beings *and* their fellow beings. Therefore their task is only to indicate how we can train our powers for collaboration in this work. Thus they place selfless dedication and the willingness to sacrifice above all other virtues. Nevertheless, they reject no one outright, for even the most egotistic can purify themselves. All the same, those seeking only for themselves—as long as they do so—will get nothing from such occultists. Even though true esotericists will never refuse to help a seeker, such seekers may well deprive themselves of the fruit of their helping guidance.

Therefore if we truly follow the instructions of a good esoteric teacher we will understand the demand that the second guardian makes after we have crossed the threshold. Indeed, if we fail to follow such a teacher's instructions we cannot expect ever to reach the threshold at all. The instructions of true esoteric teachers lead to the good, or they lead to nothing. To guide us to egotistic salvation and mere existence in the supersensible world is not their task. On the contrary, their task, from the start, is to keep us at a distance from the supra-earthly world until we can enter it with a will dedicated to full and selfless collaboration.

Appendices

Rudolf Steiner placed his work at the service and under the aegis of the Archangel Michael who, since 1879, has been the ruling spirit of earthly evolution. Toward the end of his life, Steiner told how souls gathered together in the spiritual world at the turn of the nineteenth century to experience "mighty, cosmic imaginations" in preparation for the new Michael Age, whose harbinger and foundation is anthroposophy. The earthly reflection of the heavenly Michael School is what historians of art, literature, and politics know as Romanticism. The following text is not by Steiner, who probably did not even know of it, but it miraculously captures the "high road" within which the meditative path of anthroposophy unfolds. Therefore it is included here. Context is all. Our meditation bears fruit according to our understanding of both its context as well as our own context. The German Jewish philosopher Franz Rosenzweig discovered the manuscript of *The Oldest System or Program of German Idealism* in a Berlin library in 1914 and published it in 1917. It was handwritten, clearly by the philosopher Hegel. The subject and treatment suggested the time when Hegel, Schelling, and the poet Hölderlin were seminarians together in Tübingen. But who actually wrote it? Though in Hegel's hand, the internal evidence was slight that he himself had written it. Probably, he had been only the copyist. Rosenzweig's guess was that Schelling was the author. Now, it seems more likely to have been Hölderlin. There is no certain answer. Hence we are justified in proposing that it originated in heaven, in the Michael School.

I

The Oldest System or Program of German Idealism

An *ethics*. Since, in the future, the whole of metaphysics will fall into morals, which Kant's two practical postulates—given only as an example—have not exhausted, this ethics will be nothing else but a complete system of all ideas or, what is the same, all practical postulates. The first idea is, naturally, the representation of *myself* as an absolutely free being. With a free self-conscious being, a whole world immediately arises *out of nothing*—as the only true and thinkable creation out of nothing. Here I will descend into the field of physics. The question is this: How must a world for a moral being be constituted? I would like to give our slow moving, laboriously experiment-dependent physics wings again.

Once philosophy provides the ideas and experience makes the facts available, we will finally be able to achieve the grand scale physics I expect in the future. It does not seem that contemporary physics can satisfy a creative spirit such as ours is—or should be. .

From nature, I turn to the work of humanity. Starting with the idea of humanity itself, I want to show that there is no idea of the state, as there is no idea of a machine, because the state is a mechanical phenomenon. Only the object of freedom may be called an idea. Hence, we must move beyond the state! Every state must treat free beings as mechanical cogs. It should not; therefore it must cease! You yourself see that, here, all ideas—of eternal peace and so on—are simply ideas that serve a higher idea.

At the same time, I want to establish the principles for a history of humanity, stripping to the skin the whole wretched human work of the state, with its constitution, its government, and its legislation.

Finally, I want to establish the ideas of a moral world, divinity, immortality—with the overthrow of all superstition, and equally of all persecution of the priesthood that recently claimed, through reason itself, reason as its ground. I want to establish the absolute freedom of all spirits who carry the intellectual world within them, seeking neither God nor immortality outside themselves.

Finally, I want to establish the idea that unites all: the idea of beauty, understood in the higher, Platonic sense. I am now convinced that the highest act of reason, since it includes all ideas, is an *aesthetic act,* and that truth and goodness are united as sisters only through beauty. Philosophers must possess as much aesthetic power as the poets do. Those without an aesthetic sense are the philosophers of literalism. The philosophy of spirit is an aesthetic philosophy. You cannot be rich in spirit in anything—you cannot even reason about history with spirit—without an aesthetic sense. Here, what people actually lack who do not understand ideas—who are honest enough to confess that everything is opaque for them once it goes beyond tables and calculations—will be revealed.

Poetry thus gains a higher value. In the end, she will become what she was to begin with—the teacher of humanity. For there will no longer be any philosophy or history. Only poetry will survive the remaining sciences and arts.

At the same time, we often hear that the multitudes must have a sensual religion. But it is not only the multitudes—philosophers, too, need a religion of the senses. Monotheism of the reason and the heart, polytheism of the imagination and of art: this is what we need.

First, I will speak of an idea that, as far as I know, has not occurred to anyone. We need a new mythology. But this mythology must serve the ideas. It must become a mythology of reason.

Until we can make ideas aesthetic — that is, mythological—they will not interest people. Conversely, until mythology becomes reasonable, philosophers will be ashamed of it. In the end, the enlightened and the unenlightened must reach out their hands to each other. Mythology must become philosophical, people must become reasonable, and philosophy must become mythological—then philosophers will become sensuous. Eternal unity will then reign among us. The contemptuous look and the blind trembling of the populace before its sages and priests will exist no more. Only then will the simultaneous building up of all powers—of the individual as well as all individuals—await us. No power will be suppressed. General freedom and equality of spirits will reign. A higher spirit sent from heaven will have to found this new religion among us. It will be humanity's last, greatest work.

II

States of Consciousness and Stages of Knowing
Imagination, Inspiration, Intuition

The traditional account describes four states of consciousness: ordinary consciousness, sleep or dream consciousness, dreamless sleep, and the fourth state. Rudolf Steiner likewise distinguishes four ways of knowing or kinds of knowledge: material, imaginative, inspirational ("of the nature of the will"), and intuitive.

In ordinary, material, sense-based knowing, four elements are involved: the *object* or sensation; the *image* (which we form of the object); the *concept* (through which we arrive at an understanding of the object or event); and the *"I"* (which forms image and concept based on the impression of the object.)

In imaginative knowledge, as in sleep, the object or sensation— the outer world—is no longer present. One is free of all sense impressions and of all understanding based upon them. In this sense, ones thinking or soul is "brain-free." Only three elements are involved: image, concept, and "I." To practice this level of knowing, we must acquire the faculty of forming—or working with— meaningful images, drawn from the depths of the soul, that are independent of sense perception and are, in fact, derived the spiritual world. Great care must be taken not to be led astray by fantasy. Steiner recommends we discriminate on the basis of the "sense of reality." If we experience the world of images as more "real" than those derived from the sense world, then they derive from a higher source.

In imaginative consciousness, the same forces are active as during ordinary consciousness, but now, instead of working through the senses, they work to create spiritual organs of perception. The soul now works no longer only on the body, but begins to work on itself.

In inspirational knowledge, images no longer appear. There are only two elements: concepts and the "I." Inspiration gives the impressions; the "I" forms the concepts. Steiner likens this world of a world of spiritual "tones" or "cosmic speech." "One begins to hear what is going on at the heart of things. The stone, the plant, and so forth, become spiritual words."

In intuitive knowledge only the "I" remains. One becomes what one knows and lives in all things—unites oneself with, and enters, other spiritual beings.

The path to heightened ways of knowing is meditation and its two wings: attention and devotion. These should be practiced assiduously, but separately. Practiced intensively, they enable us to separate soul from body and first rise to imagination, then inspiration, and finally intuition. For Rudolf Steiner these four ways of knowing represent a more or less natural progression in the process of spiritual cognition. Taken together, they are they represent *the fullness and wholeness of our human capacity to know.* Though it is certainly preferable to work patiently and consistently, developing each level or stage in turn, they do not constitute any kind of rigid sequence and, in fact, we can enter one at any time. "States exist and men pass through them," wrote William Blake. Anyone practicing meditation—attention and devotion—will always have experiences "out of sequence." However, for a grounded practice, one will do well, as Plato was said to have warned and Steiner always taught, "not go too quickly from the many to the one."

III

A final word from Rudolf Steiner

If one practices an inner exercise of thinking concentration long enough, one gradually comes to realize that one has entered soul experiences that separate the soul from all processes of thinking and ideation bound to physical organs. The same realization can occur in relation to feeling and willing, and even sensation or the perception of outer things. But one can achieve something on this path only if one is not afraid to admit that self-knowledge cannot be gained by mere introspection, which is always available, but rather only through what one discovers through soul work on the inner life and thus is revealed only by these exercises.

Through continued practice or soul work that is, by holding the attention on the activity of thinking, feeling and willing, these experiences in a certain way become spiritually "condensed." They grow thicker and stronger in themselves. In this state of "thickening" they reveal their inner nature that cannot be perceived in ordinary consciousness. Through such exercises, one discovers how in order to achieve ordinary consciousness our soul forces are so "thinned" that they become imperceptible in their "thinness." The soul exercises consist in the *unlimited intensification* and increase of faculties that are known to ordinary consciousness, but usually never reach such a state of intensification. The faculties are *attention* and *loving surrender to the content of the souls experience*. To attain the aim, these abilities must be intensified to such a degree that they function as entirely new soul forces.

—*The Riddles of Philosophy*

Bibliography, Further Reading, and Sources

Barnes, Henry, *A Life for the Spirit: Rudolf Steiner in the Crosscurrents of Our Time*, Great Barrington, MA: Anthroposophic Press, 1997.

Karl König, Karl, *The Inner Path*, Botton Village: Camphill Book, 1994

———, *Rudolf Steiner's Calendar of the Soul: A Commentary*, London: Rudolf Steiner Press 198.

Kühlewind, Georg, *From Normal to Healthy: Paths to the Liberation of Consciousness*, Great Barrington, MA: Lindisfarne Books, 1988.

———, *Meditation and the Soft Will*, Great Barrington, MA: Lindisfarne Books, 2003.

Lipson, Michael, *Stairway of Surprise: Six Steps to a Creative Life*, Great Barrington, MA: Lindisfarne Books, 2002.

Lowndes, Florin, *Enlivening the Chakra of the Heart: The Fundamental Spiritual Exercises of Rudolf Steiner*, London: Sophia Books, 1998.

Rittelmeyer, Friedrich, *Meditation*, Edinburgh: Floris Books 1936.

Schiller, Paul Eugen, *Rudolf Steiner and Initiation*, Spring Valley: Anthroposophic Press, 1981.

Smit, Jorgen, *How to Transform Thinking, Feeling, and Willing*, Stroud: Hawthorne Books, 1998.

Steiner, Rudolf, *Anthroposophical Leading Thoughts: Anthroposophy As a Path of Knowledge—The Michael Mystery*, London: Rudolf Steiner Press, 1973.

———, *Anthroposophy and the Inner Life*, London: Rudolf Steiner Press, 1994.

———, *Autobiography: Chapters from the Course of My Life, 1861–1907*, Great Barrington, MA: Anthroposophic Press, 1999.

———, *Christ and the Spiritual World, The Search for the Holy Grail*, London: Rudolf Steiner Press, 1963.

———, *Christianity As Mystical Fact*, Great Barrington, MA: Anthroposophic Press, 1997.

———, *The Effects of Esoteric Development*, Great Barrington, MA: Anthroposophic Press, 1997.

————, *Esoteric Development: Lectures and Writings*, Great Barrington, MA: SteinerBooks, 2003.

————, *First Steps in Inner Development*, Great Barrington, MA: Anthroposophic Press, 1999.

————, *Founding a Science of the Spirit*, London: Rudolf Steiner Press, 1999.

————, *Four Mystery Dramas: The Portal of Initiation, The Soul's Probation, The Guardian of the Threshold, The Soul's Awakening*, London: Rudolf Steiner Press, 1997.

————, *From the History & Contents of the History and Contents of the First Section of the Esoteric School, 1904–1914*, Great Barrington, MA: Anthroposophic Press, 1998. (Includes Rudolf Steiner's "Exegesis to *Light on the Path* by Mabel Collins.")

————, *Goethe's World View*, Spring Valley: Mercury Press, 1985.

————, *Guidance in Esoteric Training: From the Esoteric School*, London: Rudolf Steiner Press, 2001.

————, *How to Know Higher Worlds: A Modern Path of Initiation*, Great Barrington, MA: Anthroposophic Press, 1994.

————, *Intuitive Thinking As a Spiritual Path: A Philosophy of Freedom*, Great Barrington, MA: Anthroposophic Press, 1995.

————, *The Last Address*, London: Rudolf Steiner Press, 1967.

————, *Mystics after Modernism: Discovering the Seeds of a New Science in the Renaissance*, Great Barrington, MA: Anthroposophic Press, 2000.

————, *Nature's Open Secret: Introductions to Goethe's Scientific Writings*, Great Barrington, MA: Anthroposophic Press, 2000.

————, *Occult Reading and Occult Hearing*, London: Rudolf Steiner Press, 1975.

————, *An Outline of Esoteric Science*, Great Barrington, MA: Anthroposophic Press, 1997.

————, *The Presence of the Dead on the Spiritual Path*, Great Barrington, MA: Anthroposophic Press, 1990.

————, *The Reappearance of Christ in the Etheric: A Collection of Lectures on the Second Coming of Christ*, Great Barrington, MA: SteinerBooks, 2003.

————, *The Redemption of Thinking*, Spring Valley: Anthroposophic Press, 1983.

————, *The Riddles of Philosophy* Spring Valley, N.Y.: Anthroposophic Press, 1973.

————, *Riddles of the Soul*, Spring Valley: Mercury Press, 1996.

————, *The Science of Knowing*, Spring Valley: Mercury Press, 1988.

————, *Secrets of the Threshold*, Hudson: Anthroposophic Press, 1987.

————, *Self-Transformation: Selected Lectures*, London: Rudolf Steiner Press, 1995.

————, *Sleep and Dreams: A Bridge to the Spirit*, Great Barrington, MA: Steiner-Books, 2003.

————, *The Souls' Probation: A Mystery Drama*, Great Barrington, MA: Anthroposophic Press, 1995.

————, *The Spiritual Foundation of Morality*, Great Barrington, MA: Anthroposophic Press, 1995.

————, *The Spiritual Guidance of the Individual and Humanity*, Great Barrington, MA: Anthroposophic Press, 1991.

————, *The Spiritual Hierarchies and the Physical World*, Hudson: Anthroposophic Press, 1996.

————, *The Stages of Higher Knowledge*, Spring Valley: Anthroposophic Press, 1967.

————, *Staying Connected: How to Continue Your Relationships with Those Who Have Died*, Great Barrington, MA: Anthroposophic Press, 1999.

————, *Theosophy: An Introduction to the Spiritual Processes in Human Life and in the Cosmos*, Great Barrington, MA: Anthroposophic Press, 1994.

————, *Truth and Knowledge*, Blauvelt, NY: Rudolf Steiner Publications, 1981.

————, *A Way of Self-Knowledge*, Great Barrington, MA: Anthroposophic Press, 1998.

————, *What Is Anthroposophy?*, Great Barrington, MA: SteinerBooks, 2002.

————, *The World of the Senses and the World of the Spirit*, Hudson: Anthroposophic Press, 1996.

Steiner, Rudolf and Steiner-von Sivers, Marie, *Correspondence and Documents, 1901–1925*, London: Rudolf Steiner Press, 1988.

Swassjan, Karin, *The Ultimate Communion of Mankind*, London: Temple Lodge, 1996.

Wachsmuth, Guenther, *The Life and Work of Rudolf Steiner: From the Turn of the Century to His Death*, Blauvelt, NY: Spiritual Science Library, 1989.

Zeylmans von Emmichover, F. W., *The Foundation Stone*, London: Rudolf Steiner Press, 1963.

SOURCES

This volume contains selections translated from the following complete works (Gesamtausgabe [GA]) of Rudolf Steiner, published by the Rudolf Steiner Nachlassverwaltung, Dornach, Switzerland:

Einleitungen zu Goethe's Naturwissenschaftlichen Schriften (GA 1). In English: *Nature's Open Secret.*

Die Philosophie der Freiheit (GA 40). In English: *Intuitive Thinking As a Spiritual Path.*

Wie erlangt man Erkenntnisse der höheren Welten (GA 10). In English: *How to Know Higher Worlds.*

Die Geheimwissenschaft im Umriss (GA 13). In English: *An Outline of Esoteric Science.*

Die Schwelle der geistigen Welt (GA 17). In English: *A Way of Self-Knowledge.*

Wahrspruchworte (GA 40). In English (selections): *Truth-Wrought Words; Verses and Meditations; Calendar of the Soul.*

Sprüche, Dichtungen, Mantren (GA 40a).

Ursprung und Ziel des Menschen (GA 53). In English (partial): *First Steps in Inner Development.*

Die Welträtsel und die Anthroposophie (GA 54). In English (partial): *First Steps in Inner Development.*

Vor der Tore der Theosophie (GA 95). In English: *Founding a Science of the Spirit.*

Anweisungen für eine esoterische Schulung (GA 245). In English: *Guidance in Esoteric Training.*

Unsere Toten (GA 261). In English (selections): *Staying Connected.*

Zur Geschichte und aus den Inhalten der ersten Abteilung der Esoterische Schule (1904–1914) (GA 264). In English: *From the History and Contents of the Esoteric School.*

Zur Geschichte und aus den Inhalten der erkenntniskultischen Abteilung der Esoterische Schule 1904–1914 (GA265).

Aus den Inhalten der Esoterischen Stunden I, II, III (GA 266/1/2/3).

Seelenübungen mit Wort- und Sinnbild-Meditationen (GA 267).

Mantrische Sprüche: Seelenübungen II (GA 268).

Acknowledgments

We would like to thank the following contributors whose donations made possible the publication of this book. Publishing Rudolf Steiner is not a commercial venture. It is a deed of cultural and spiritual service that we cannot do alone, but only with the continued help and support of those who recognize its importance and value.

If you would like to contribute to the work and help make available another book by Rudolf Steiner, please write to us at: SteinerBooks, 610 Main Street, Great Barrington, MA 01230.

Anonymous (69)
Paul Abatsis
Christopher O. Allen
RoseannaAlmaee
Alfred & Martha Bartles
Candace & Charles Coffin
Jonathan Davidson
Marilyn & Donald Shanks
Patty & Steve Eikam
Charles & Elaine H. Bily
Ann S. Finucane
Susan M. Graesser
Annie & DillonGray
Jay & Lori Harms
Cathy Hart
David Kessling
Lee & John Lecraw
Cornelia Logan
Louise Ann Ludford
Mary Mangano
Brian H. Manning
Jane Martindale
Sharron Burruss Massie
Edward B. McCabe

Davina Muse
Jeanne Noble
Robert W. Nuckels
Fruzan Parvanta
Eleanor G. Paul
Michael Pojanowski
Jim Rimbey
Juliet Roby
Sara Genta Romero
Joel & Alana Ronningen
Heather Ross
Olivia Salazar
Ruta Sepetys
H. Reid Shaw
Sybil Shearer
Jeff Stacey
Martha Starkey
Mark R. Webb
Michael White
Elaine K.F. White
Wilhelm Wuellner
Walter M. Yost
& Rives Rea Yost